PRACTICAL STRATEGIES FOR PARENTING YOUR CHILD WITH ADHD

DAILY STEPS TO NURTURE YOUR CHILD, FOSTER HEALTHY RELATIONSHIPS,

AND DEVELOP BEHAVIORAL SKILLS TO THRIVE!

THOMAS AND CARRIE ALLEN

SHADE TREE
— PUBLISHING —

Table of Contents

To our beautiful children. We love you to the moon and back!

Love,

Mom and Dad

THANK YOU!

Thanks for buying this book! The link below will take you to our Linktree where you will find links to our books, social media pages, and the FREE downloadable worksheets that come with this purchase. If you choose to subscribe, we promise to only email with the chance to get our next book free during a limited promotion.

As advertised with our book, the link will take you to the **FREE GIFT** : over 20 downloadable worksheets you can use to help your child improve their executive functioning skills. From attention and emotional regulation to social skills and choosing good friends.

Click here or type this address into your web browser to download your FREE worksheets: https://linktr.ee/adhdparenting

We would love to hear from you! Use the link above to contact us any time with questions or to be included in our next promotion. Again, thank you so much for buying our book! We hope it helps you, your child, and your whole family!

Introduction

Raising a child with attention-deficit/hyperactivity disorder (ADHD) requires parents to be more hands-on in teaching their children essential life skills. Many parenting books can be frustrating because the strategies don't work for your child. Your goal as a parent is to get your child to a place of independence, but the road to get there will have many curves and roadblocks. Parents play a key role in helping kids with ADHD succeed. And for parents who are also neurodivergent, the strategies in this book can help you and your child simultaneously. Our approach is based on these ideas:

- You cannot parent from a place of chaos and overwhelm. It's harder to respond calmly when you are stressed out. So, you will need structure and systems in place in your home to parent effectively. You also need to focus on your own mental and physical health.
- Setting realistic expectations instead of focusing on how you hoped parenthood would be will help you enjoy the family you are part of.

- Training parents to interact effectively with their children is one of the most significant ways to help families.
- Children with ADHD learn best in the moment. The best time to teach your child skills is when they are doing an activity requiring those skills during everyday life. It is harder to learn in a social skills group or therapy session and then apply it.

Expect to see changes over time. Slow but steady improvements are what to look for. If you use the activities in this book, you will be able to see the progress your child is making by observing a decrease in undesirable behaviors. Don't get discouraged if you aren't seeing quick results; kids with ADHD are brilliant. You might even see an increase in undesirable behaviors as they test to see how serious you are and how consistent you will be.

Raising a neurodivergent child can be chaotic. Every day offers something new—a rush to get out the door, forgotten homework assignments, and a radiant child bursting with energy and love for the world around them. You have a unique child and love them dearly, but sometimes, you don't know what to do or how to parent them.

It doesn't have to be this way—you can enjoy the positives of parenting while growing from the negatives and improving your (and your child's) life. How amazing would it feel to watch your child become increasingly more independent and overcome the challenges caused by their ADHD?

You might find it overwhelming when you step back to think about your child's behavior, listing out the most troubling among them. It can seem like your child is just misbehaving as if they don't respect you, don't *want* to respect you, or can't find the will to be one of those kids who seem so put together. Coming to this realization can be frustrating and misguided. At first, it is hard to understand that your child isn't "acting out" and that many of those behavioral problems can be tied back to their ADHD.

Even if you know this, understanding the link between ADHD and behavioral problems doesn't free you from what it feels like to be a parent with these issues. Beyond merely feeling a lack of respect, you may feel stressed—in a society that expects your child to behave in specific ways, how do you rein in these behaviors? Moreover, public episodes and tantrums can feel embarrassing, like others are judging you as a parent for your child's behavior.

The fact of the matter is that for children with ADHD, skills like emotional regulation, self-control, organization, and even social skills like listening don't come naturally. That's not to say a child with ADHD can't have these skills, but they may need a bit of help getting to that stage. And that's where your help comes in:

- Learning how to teach your child executive skills like staying focused
- Keeping track of time, planning, and organizing.
- Keeping their cool for seemingly random and insignificant incidents.

What works for neurotypical parenting doesn't always work for kids with ADHD. You have the opportunity to play a hands-on role in raising your child uniquely—all it takes is building the skills necessary to understand what your child needs and how to implement parenting tactics for success.

Have you ever read a self-help book that inspired you and left you so optimistic, only to feel overwhelmed and unsure where to start? Our hope for this book is to provide you with practical strategies to help create the peaceful home and happy family you desire and that the questions and activities at the end of each chapter help you take those first steps towards putting them into action. Change doesn't happen overnight. Instead, it is done consistently through many small steps.

After reading this book, we hope you will gain insights into understanding your child's unique ADHD brain and learn practical strategies for teaching discipline, fostering positive relationships, and instilling good behavior. Utilizing these strategies will give you a great start on enhancing your child's quality of life, preparing them for adulthood, and building a strong, supportive family unit, ensuring a happier, healthier, and more harmonious family life.

Who are we? We are parents of neurodivergent kids just like you – one of us also has ADHD. When we began our parenting journey, we were frustrated that all the parenting books weren't helping us. Utilizing my background in school counseling, I started researching best practices for children with ADHD. I spoke to speech therapists, occupational therapists, teachers, and other parents about what they thought were the most effective strategies. Once we started using these strategies, we finally noticed improvements in our children's behavior, increased independence, and less frustration.

One last word for all parents of children with ADHD:

You are *not* a bad parent! You are *not* failing your child! You *don't* have to do this alone. You *will* get through these difficult times, and your child is going to be O.K.!

It is time to embark on this journey of parenting our children with strength, courage, and resilience. Let's get started!

Chapter 1 – Understanding ADHD and How it Impacts Daily Life

"Why fit in when you were born to stand out?" —Dr. Seuss

How would you feel if teachers or coaches overlooked your child's potential because of a misunderstanding of their ability to perform? Unfortunately, this is a reality for many parents and children, even today. The discovery and diagnosis of ADHD have come a long way, even in just the last 50 years. Doctors used to label some of the symptoms as attention deficit disorder (ADD), but overly active children were not diagnosed this way if they did not display inattentive characteristics. The term hyperactivity was not included in the definition until the 1980s.

The real irony is that the disorder is *NOT* a deficit in attention, as the name would suggest. You probably notice your child hyper-focusing (sometimes to the point of hyper-fixating) on something they enjoy, which is the opposite of an attention deficit. I once heard it said that ADHD doesn't mean a child doesn't know what to do; it is that they have a problem doing what they know.

This chapter will introduce symptoms associated with ADHD, the diagnosis process, how it presents itself along with other disorders, and other essential knowledge to help you navigate the world of ADHD and support your child's journey through toddlerhood, school age, and adolescence.

Definition, Symptoms, and Diagnosis

ADHD stands for Attention Deficit / Hyperactivity Disorder. It is a neurodevelopmental disorder involving persistent patterns of inattention, hyperactivity and impulsivity, and emotional dysregulation that can significantly impact your child's daily functioning and development. Neurodevelopmental disorders are a group of disorders that develop in childhood and affect the brain's development of neurological pathways. These include ADHD, Autism Spectrum Disorder (ASD), Intellectual Disorder, and Learning Disabilities.

Though ADHD itself is not a learning disability, many people with ADHD have learning-related difficulties. According to the American Psychiatric Association (APA) Diagnostics and Statistics Manual (DSM), a learning disability is a disorder that negatively affects one's ability to acquire skills related to reading, writing, spelling, math, etc.

Myth: ADHD isn't a real disorder; it is an excuse. Everyone has those symptoms.

Reality: Scientific research has discovered significant differences in brain structure, connectivity, and neurochemistry than that of non-ADHD patients. The American Psychiatric Association (APA), the Center for Disease Control and Prevention (CDC), and the National Institutes of Health (NIH) all categorize ADHD as a medical disorder.

Conversely, ADHD does not directly impact the development of specific academic skills; it affects executive functions such as focusing, sitting still, and prioritizing information.

The Three Types of ADHD

Doctors group the symptoms of ADHD into three categories based on their presentation: inattention, hyperactivity, and impulsivity. Additionally, one's symptoms within these categories can vary with age, gender, and background. Your child might have a unique blend of the three presentations, making their experience different from their peers.

- **Predominantly Inattentive**: A child struggles mostly with attention-related symptoms such as seeming like they are always daydreaming, misplacing belongings often, overlooking details, making careless mistakes, and forgetting what they learned in school that day. Again, it is interesting that children with ADHD are not short on attention; their brains are paying attention to just about everything around them! It is more correct to say they have inconsistent attention.

- **Predominantly Hyperactive-Impulsive** is another presentation of ADHD. Children with this type may feel the urge to fidget constantly and may be more likely to interrupt others. They are continually restless, talk too much, and don't think before they act. For those around them, their behavior can seem rude--but to the child, it feels like they are bursting with energy. Often, the child is so uncomfortable that

> **Myth**: Kids with ADHD cannot focus or pay attention at all. It must be a learning disability.
>
> **Reality**: On the contrary, kids with ADHD tend to hyperfocus on activities that they find interesting. They may struggle with sustained attention on tasks that are less stimulating or require more effort, but it is important to note that this is not by choice!

they must move to get that energy out. Children with predominantly hyperactive-impulsive ADHD cannot restrain impulses nor judge conversations well, which means that they can only cope with this via jumping, running, interrupting, and emotional outbursts.

- **Combined Presentation:** Involves all the symptoms mentioned above at once. However, some children with combined presentation may still be more prone to experiencing one or the other. Children with combined presentation are the typical image one thinks of when imagining a child with ADHD.

The signs and symptoms of ADHD can also fluctuate throughout the day. Fatigue, stress, and other factors can make symptoms prominent, with many children becoming more hyperactive during the evening.

What is it Like to Have ADHD?

ADHD is a brain disorder involving specific chemicals (neurotransmitters) and structures, most notably the pre-frontal cortex. This part of the brain tends to develop slower than other children's. A lack of dopamine or norepinephrine and reduced activity in the pre-frontal cortex can contribute to a lack of executive function skills. These are skills we take for granted as adults because we use them regularly throughout our day without thinking, such as planning, prioritizing, time management, inhibition, self-motivation, organization, juggling multiple tasks, and transitioning from one task to another.

Myth: My child can't possibly have ADHD; they aren't even hyperactive. Isn't that what defines them? It is even in the name.

Reality: ADHD comes in a variety of presentations This misconception is the number one reason why so many girls do not get an ADHD diagnosis.

Children with ADHD experience dysfunction with these skills. Although not an official diagnosis, some label this as executive function deficit or disorder (EFD) because it affects many of the brain's management functions, including:

Executive Function Deficits in Children with ADHD

ADHD also includes difficulty with social skills and emotional regulation, which are not always associated with ADHD due to a focus on the three types. They will also find it hard to prioritize because kids with ADHD lack a sense of what makes things important. They have difficulty choosing between alternatives, making it seem as if they are unmotivated to do anything other than what they think is fun (preferred activities).

> **Myth**: Your kid is just lazy; he needs to try harder—or he needs stronger parenting to motivate him.
>
> **Reality**: ADHD affects the brain's ability to regulate executive function. Kids with ADHD can be highly motivated when they are "in the zone."

On the flip side, kids with ADHD will hyper-focus on something they are interested in, to the point where when they are *in the zone*, you can't get their attention to pull them away from it. Think about the ramifications of this in the school setting: teachers expect your child to do well in school for six or seven different subjects. We may only get that good in one area in the workforce. The ability to hyperfocus can be a gift for a person with ADHD who can hyper-focus on it and become a subject matter expert.

Other examples of ADHD symptoms are showing a lack of self-restraint or an ability to calm themselves down. They will feel more overwhelmed or frustrated by stressful situations than other kids. They may lose their belongings and get distracted easily, unable to string actions together to follow simple directions. These challenges can lead to the child experiencing burnout with demanding tasks.

In a classroom environment, these struggles can lead to distracting other students, fidgeting, blurting out when others speak, or failing to take turns. A child may talk too much, leave their seat without permission, or get upset because someone else is taking too long. Many times, teachers will have to pay more attention to a child with ADHD because they need to have tasks broken down for them or require visual aids to complete tasks that other students their age do not.

Time management can be one of the most difficult challenges they face. They will delay initiating or completing tasks because they have yet to learn the skills to plan and prioritize. This is *time blindness*—an inability to perceive how much time has passed, how much time they have to complete an assignment, how much time they have spent on an activity, and how to sequence steps in the correct order.

It is also important to understand that ADHD can be a lifelong disorder, but many adults learn skills to manage the struggles ADHD brings. If your child has ADHD, then they will almost specifically still have it as an adult. Studies show that "two-thirds of youth with ADHD will continue to have impairing symptoms of ADHD in adulthood."

Myth: Children with ADHD will outgrow it with time. Eating better and getting lots of exercise can solve it.

Reality: ADHD is a lifelong condition that often persists into adolescence and adulthood. While symptoms may change over time, and can improve with better lifestyle choices, many people continue to face challenges related to attention, impulsivity, and hyperactivity throughout their lives. Experts recommend treatment including medications and behavioral interventions.

Although you may notice that as your child gets older, ADHD is less prevalent in their expression because ADHD can change over time, going from one end of the spectrum to the other and even becoming more internalized—both due to treatment and societal pressures.

Even though studies are showing an increase in diagnosis in adults, most adults with ADHD will not display outward hyperactive behavior but will be internally hyperactive. They will still deal with restlessness, boredom, irritability, racing thoughts, and impulsiveness, leading to mental fatigue and burnout—but this can be managed by developing proper skills.

Adults with ADHD may also describe being stuck in the now, unable to look to the future or even learn from the past. Because they live *in the now*, they are typically more intense, live more passionately, and usually more overwhelmed by life events.

What Causes ADHD?

The exact cause of ADHD is not clear. We know it involves specific neurotransmitters imbalances—chemical messengers in the brain—such as dopamine and norepinephrine. Still, we do not truly know why those neurotransmitters are imbalanced in the first place.

The DSM helps us understand that ADHD is a description of the symptoms and not an explanation for them. That said, there is a lot of research indicating that there is a genetic component to ADHD. Studies of twins and their families have shown that genetic factors cause around 75%-90% of ADHD in these children. Close to 50% of parents who have ADHD have a child with the disorder.

Other causes include under-development or injury to the brain and risks from a mother's use of alcohol and tobacco during pregnancy. However, scientific studies do not support the theory that ADHD is caused by technology use, too much sugar consumption, or bad parenting. Although not identified as a direct cause, scientists have also found links to ADHD and exposure to neurotoxins:

- **Lead** disrupts digestion, interferes with the body's central nervous system, and impairs humans' respiratory and reproductive systems.
- **Polychlorinated Biphenyls (PCBs)**: shown to cause cancer and several serious non-cancer health effects on the immune system, reproductive system, nervous system, and endocrine system.; and
- **Bisphenol A (BPAs)**: a chemical used to manufacture plastics that can accumulate in organs.

How Is ADHD Diagnosed?

The diagnosis of ADHD has changed over the years. The first documented cases were described in the late 1700s as an attention disease where children were born with an unhealthy level of distractibility that some children are born with. In the late 1800s and early 1900s, doctors noted impulsivity, lack of self-restraint, and motor restlessness; the condition wasn't an impairment of intellect or physical disease, and it seemed to affect more boys than girls.

It was the mid-1930s when doctors began prescribing medication for behavior disorders. They discovered that stimulants produced better focus and a decrease in motor activity in children with short attention spans, hyperactivity, impulsiveness, mood disability, and poor memory.

> **Myth**: ADHD is a result of your parenting style.
>
> **Reality**: Environmental factors and parenting styles can influence symptom severity, but they are specifically not the root cause. Research shows that ADHD has a genetic component based on chemical and structural differences in the brain.

Much more is known today, which makes the diagnosis of ADHD straightforward. By the time a child is around six years old, usually before, the parents have become aware that their child is showing inattention, increased motor activity, and impulsiveness. Healthcare providers turn to the guidelines in the DSM version 5, published in 2022, which provides criteria used to diagnose a child when ADHD is suspected:

- **Inattention**: For children up to age 16, 6+ symptoms of inattention must be present; for those 17 and older, 5+ symptoms must be present. The symptoms of inattention have to have persisted for at least six months and are markedly inappropriate for the individual's development level.
- **Hyperactivity and impulsivity**: The exact number of symptoms for each age group persists, but the symptoms must be present for six or more months and prove disruptive to one's life compared to their developmental level.

Despite the criteria seeming relatively simple, it is essential that if you believe that your child has ADHD, you take them to get a professional opinion, as this is a gateway to getting proper support and treatment for their needs.

ADHD in Boys vs. Girls

The presentation of ADHD can often be different in boys and girls. Of the 6.1 million American children with diagnosed ADHD, most are boys (Jones, 2023). Specifically, 12.9% of boys compared to 5.6% of girls.

When you think of ADHD, you most likely have an image of a child bouncing off the walls, fidgeting, and not remembering details. This stereotypical image of ADHD is more suited to how boys experience ADHD; it is outward and obvious, which leads to a higher rate of diagnosis. On the other hand, girls tend to experience

Myth: Girls don't get ADHD; only boys have it.

Reality: More boys indeed tend to have ADHD than girls, by more than half. But that means girls can have it too, and it is more helpful to focus on identifying whether or not your child shows signs of executive function deficits than whether their gender is a factor.

inattentive symptoms that seem like depression and anxiety, often resulting in fewer ADHD diagnoses and even misdiagnosis (with depression and anxiety being commonly confused for female ADHD).

Varying studies show that after the age of approximately seven, males with hyperactive or impulsive ADHD tend to calm down, developing more prominent inattention or unconscious suppression of hyperactive and impulsive symptoms. As male children age, they produce less estrogen and ultimately *simmer down*. However, because female children gain estrogen, this can result in symptoms increasing after the age of seven. Moreover, puberty-related hormonal shifts, like pre-menstrual estrogen increases, can make it hard to discern ADHD from regular mood swings.

You should look out for both inattention and hyperactivity symptoms across all ages and genders, especially if you have ADHD. If you believe your daughter has ADHD and professionals give you the runaround, do not be afraid to advocate for her and get a second opinion, as misdiagnosis and medical neglect are severe issues for females with ADHD.

Comorbidities

Any disorder occurring alongside another disorder is called a comorbidity. In children with ADHD, comorbid conditions can influence the progression and presentation of symptoms, as well as the available treatment options. For example, many children with ADHD also experience Autism Spectrum Disorder (ASD). Studies show that 57% of females with Autism will also receive an ADHD diagnosis; 49% of males with Autism are diagnosed with ADHD. These numbers do not even account for the fact that ASD often goes undiagnosed and that everyone with the two disorders does not have any diagnosis. As a result of this comorbidity,

> Studies found that 57% of females and 49% of males with Autism will also receive an ADHD diagnosis.

your child could struggle with communication, anxiety, depression, and other intersecting symptoms.

Also, children with ADHD are more likely to have poor mental health than those with ASD alone. Some experts believe that the increased stress and expectations placed upon children with ADHD—specifically when it comes to conforming—can heighten the risk of developing such disorders.

Our son has an extreme sensitivity to light, sound, texture, and other sensory input, which can be so overwhelming to him that he has to actively drown it out. For example, when he was two years old, he would hum while eating. Family members would laugh, thinking he was just really enjoying his food! However, as he grew older, he told us it is because the chewing noise is so loud that it drowns out his other senses.

He used to absolutely freak out if his face got wet, or when the dentist would want to look in his mouth, or even throw a tantrum if a nurse used an otoscope (those devices they use to look in your ear canal). He even hates having his head scratched because it is "too loud." He enjoys the feeling, but because the sensory input is overwhelming, he would rather not experience it. He has to work hard to drown out the sensory input, whereas you and I can sometimes self-regulate without even thinking about it.

ADHD is also commonly comorbid with anxiety and depression. Up to 30% of kids with ADHD also have a mood-related disorder like depression, and about 25% of kids with ADHD have a distinct anxiety disorder.

We learned this is called **Sensory Processing Disorder** (SPD), and is common among children with ADHD and Autism. SPD is when our brain has difficulty processing information it receives through the senses; almost as if the light is always too bright; sounds are always too loud, clothes are always too itchy, and smells are always too stinky, all at the same time. Often, children with ADHD "meltdown" for seemingly unknown reasons, which can be due to a hypersensitivity to sensory input that you and I would not notice but can feel overbearing to your child. In other cases, a child may feel wholly numb or desensitized to sensory input. This dysregulation of sensory processing can cause a child to feel "irritated, distracted, or even saddened by how something sounds, feels, looks, or tastes."

Many children with ADHD also suffer from something called **Oppositional Defiant Disorder** (ODD), which often involves persistent patterns of defiant, disobedient, and hostile behavior. It commonly coexists with ADHD, as impulsivity and difficulty with authority figures may contribute to oppositional behaviors. Just under half of kids with ADHD also have ODD. Something to note about ODD is that medication is usually NOT the first treatment recommended. Typically, a doctor will suggest other behavioral therapies rather than prescribing medication.

Since learning disabilities often accompany ADHD, it explains why many people incorrectly assume that ADHD is a learning disability itself. As mentioned, the DSM-5-TR, the ADD, and other leading authorities in psychology and medicine do not consider ADHD a learning disability; instead, they categorize it as a neurodevelopmental disorder. However, some common learning disabilities are co-morbid with ADHD, meaning they can exist alongside ADHD. These include:

- **Dyslexia** is a learning disability associated with reading that can cause comprehension, spelling, and writing difficulties.
- **Dyscalculia** is when a person has difficulty understanding numbers and performing arithmetic.
- **Dysgraphia** makes it difficult for someone to write, affecting their handwriting and ability to put thoughts onto paper.

These disabilities can impact the ability of kids with ADHD to interpret written language, including math, handwriting, imagery, and simple literature. These problems are especially troublesome in an academic environment.

Why Comorbidities Matter

Understanding which disorders can occur alongside ADHD is essential for developing a holistic treatment plan that examines all areas of your child's mental health rather than addressing isolated symptoms. In other words, treating comorbid conditions ensures that your child receives comprehensive care that considers the interconnected nature of mental health and developmental disorders.

Additionally, treating comorbid conditions can ensure that your child has a higher quality of life. Undiagnosed and untreated comorbidities can result in higher levels of stress and self-esteem issues, as well as lower levels of resilience.

It also allows for enhanced, targeted treatment that prevents symptoms from worsening over time. With awareness of other conditions that are often present alongside ADHD, you can start the process of treatment early, empowering your child to live their best life while embracing their unique personality traits—as opposed to condemning parts of themselves due to ADHD.

Key Takeaways from this Chapter

The main points we want you to leave this chapter knowing are:

1. ADHD is a neurological disorder that affects a child's brain, distinguished by differences in brain structure and neurotransmitters.

2. ADHD itself is NOT a learning disability; however, statistics show that learning disabilities will often accompany the symptoms of ADHD.

3. ADHD has three presentations: Inattentive, Hyperactive-Impulsive, and Combined presentation. Your child will most likely display one of these three: how a doctor will diagnose their situation.

4. Children with ADHD experience dysfunction in their ability to control and manage their cognitive skills and behaviors.

5. The exact cause of ADHD is unknown; however, scientific research has shown that there is a significant genetic component to ADHD.

6. ADHD will often occur alongside another disorder which sometimes makes accurate diagnosis difficult.

ACTIVITY: Analyzing Your Child's Behavior: Part I

The following activity will help you identify concerning behaviors and recognize the exceptional strengths of your child. We will build upon these insights in Chapter 5.

1. **Behaviors of concern:**

    A. Take a moment to reflect on specific behaviors that have been challenging to you. These could be related to impulsivity, inattention, hyperactivity, or any other aspect of behavior that is concerning you.

    B. List these behaviors in the worksheet below or create your own. Be specific and describe situations and settings where these behaviors are more prominent.

2. **Exceptional strengths:**

    A. Now, focus on your child's exceptional strengths, positive qualities, and where your child shines, shows resilience, or demonstrates unique talents.

    B. List these strengths in the worksheet. Highlight situations, settings, or activities where these strengths become apparent.

3. **Reflection:**

    A. Take a moment to reflect on your child's dual nature—both challenging behaviors and the exceptional strengths.

    B. Consider how understanding these behaviors and strengths can pave the way for effective strategies and interventions.

Next, use an ABC chart over the next week to record problem behaviors. An ABC chart captures the following:

*   **Antecedent**: what is occurring before a behavior
*   **Behavior:** the actual behavior itself
*   **Consequence**: what happened directly after the behavior

When recording the antecedent, consider the time of day, any changes to their routine, other people present, and anything else that may have influenced their behavior. The objective is to identify patterns and causes of behaviors. The consequences include getting attention from a parent, getting something they want, getting something taken away, or being ignored. This shouldn't be misunderstood as punishment they receive for their behavior. Make sure you record how your child responds to the consequence as well. Does the situation escalate or de-escalate?

Try to add more data, such as the setting, how your child responds to you, any comments on how it affected others, etc. You can create either worksheet on a blank piece of paper, a notepad, or a spreadsheet program on your computer. It doesn't need to be ours. We provided these as examples to help you capture data. Be sure to record the time of day, place, or environmental circumstances so they can identify patterns.

Example ABC Chart

Time	Setting	Antecedent	Behavior	Consequence
8:26 am	Getting ready for school	Brother came in to brush his teeth	Screamed at him to get out	An argument ensued, and parents had to get involved
9:10 am	Eating breakfast	The dog ate her bacon	She started kicking the dog and continued after being told to stop	It Started the morning off badly with more screaming and misbehavior
11:30 am	Eating lunch	Mom asked her to stop playing her video game and focus on eating.	She ignored Mom and got upset	Mom repeated the but she started yelling and did not eat.
2:17 pm	Playing with sibling	Brother grabbed toy	Screamed at him and tried to hit him	Brother left, yelling about not wanting to play with her anymore
4:14 pm	Asking for ice cream right before dinner	Mom said, "No."	She began to scream and throw a fit.	She received negative attention from her father.

Chapter 2 – Treatment Approaches for ADHD

"Strength does not come from winning. Your struggles develop your strengths. When you go through hardships and decide not to surrender, that is strength."

—Gandhi

O ne of the best steps you can take is learning your child's available treatment options. Every child's presentation of ADHD is different, so they will require customized treatment; which is why understanding your child's behavior and possible comorbidities is also vital.

Although doctors and therapists use various methods to address the symptoms and deficits of ADHD, we do not intend for this chapter to be a comprehensive list of all the techniques used. We won't be describing any experimental treatments or therapies. We aim to discuss evidence-based treatments and some additional supplemental-type therapies (i.e., not intended to be the sole source of treatment). Evidence-based treatments have undergone significant scientific research, which has determined that this treatment is effective for the condition it was intended to treat.

Before we dive into the various treatment options available, let's talk about how to measure progress. Most therapists and coaches like to follow data-driven approaches to identify trends and gauge progress. All this means is that they will use metrics such as an observed symptom or behavior, the date and time of day observed, the severity or frequency of the behavior, etc. By measuring these metrics, a therapist can determine whether specific treatment methods are effective or should be adjusted to achieve the desired result. Using the ABC chart, you can also monitor this data to discover trends and gauge your child's progress with various behaviors, such as mood swings or executive functioning skill deficits.

Meeting Basic Needs First

Ok, this section will not be a Parenting 101 discussion. However, it is worth mentioning some basics for parenting a child with ADHD while incorporating treatments, whether behavioral or pharmacological. When evaluating our children's needs, we must understand that basic needs such as proper sleep, regular exercise, a healthy diet, and routines and structure in the home are crucial to see maximum progress. Areas that are essential to get correct before we move up to harder tasks like teaching organizational skills or time management. If your child is sleep deprived, all the organization skills in the world will not help them complete a difficult assignment or control their emotions.

Behavioral Parent Training

Let's talk about what can be one of the most beneficial treatment options you should consider for your child. It is called Behavioral Parent Training (BPT), and this form of treatment emphasizes the essential role parents play in helping their children with ADHD. The objective of BPT is to coach parents on strategies to mitigate their children's self-regulation challenges. More specifically, we mean challenges related to working memory limitations, slower cognitive processing, difficulty waiting, and the ability to resist doing something they want to do.

<u>The CDC recommends BPT before medication, especially whenever:</u>

- The child is under six, or the diagnosis is not specific.
- Parents prefer to try therapy over medication.
- The child has a comorbid conduct disorder such as ODD.

The primary emphasis of BPT is on coaching parents to consistently use positive reinforcement and fewer reprimands, create structure at home, create boundaries, and practice proper parental self-care. For example, you may notice your child may modify their behavior to avoid punishment. Children with ADHD respond better to reinforcement rather than reprimands. Therefore, your role is to learn skills and establish structure in your household. You will create daily routines, learn to use more specific language while giving direction, and chunk large tasks into smaller, more manageable goals. You should establish age-appropriate "house rules" to provide clear expectations of what behaviors are *undesirable* and clear consequences for breaking them.

The American Academy of Pediatrics (AAP) says that 45% of preschoolers with ADHD receive behavior therapy before being prescribed medication.

Key Benefits of Behavioral Parent Training

- Fostering a healthy parent-child relationship and increasing positive reinforcement rather than negative punishments
- Establishing a structured household, daily routines, and maintaining consistent parenting and discipline techniques.

- Improving executive functioning skills by prioritizing undesirable behaviors and focusing on one at a time

Ask your pediatrician for a referral if you are interested in parent training. Find a therapist that focuses on the above areas and encourages regular meetings to evaluate the family's progress. There are several BPT resources to help you and your child find a good fit. Visit sites such as CHADD.org and EffectiveChildTherapy.org for a list of referrals and questions to ask the therapist before you choose one. Ensure their plan is *evidence-based* and focuses on parent training. You can also search ABPP.org for board-certified psychologists who use evidence-based behavioral treatments.

Medication: Understanding the Pros and Cons

Whether medication is right for your child is a question only you can answer. Some experts feel medication is not meant for every case of ADHD. Interesting, while the AAP recommends behavior therapy as the first treatment for children under six, the CDC reports that 75% of children with ADHD world-wide get medical treatment and nothing else.

Please understand our position, medication has improved the lives of many people, transforming ADHD from a significant struggle to a manageable condition. Studies have concluded that medication can statistically reduce accidental injuries, substance abuse, depression, criminal activity, and other unwanted effects of untreated ADHD. Therefore, we suggest that you consider pros and cons of medicating your child and speaking with their doctor before making a decision.

Some of the benefits of ADHD medications include:

- **Enhanced cognitive function**: Many ADHD medications, and stimulants especially, can improve cognitive functions in children with ADHD, which means that they can enhance your child's ability to focus, remember, and engage on a cognitive level.

- **Behavioral regulation**: Medication can help children with ADHD manage impulsive behaviors and reduce hyperactivity.
- **Academic performance**: Children who take ADHD medications notice marked improvements in their academic achievement due to the ability to focus and engage easier.
- **Enhanced social functioning**: Medication may also improve social skills and interactions with other children their age.
- **Quality of life**: Medication can improve the overall quality of life children with ADHD experience in terms of everyday functioning and task facilitation.

On the other hand, we would be remiss if we did not mention some of the potential downsides of ADHD medications as well:

- Some ADHD medications can cause side effects like insomnia, decreased appetite, and irritable mood. A doctor can eliminate these by adjusting the medication dosage or combination.
- With stimulant medications, one might experience cardiovascular risks that require careful monitoring.

Myth: ADHD medicine has too many side effects for it to be worth giving to my child.

Reality: Regulatory agencies confirm that several ADHD medications are safe with minimal side effects, which a doctor can manage by changing dosage or medication. In fact, non-medicinal treatments have can be less effective unless combined with medication.

- ADHD medications only offer temporary relief, which means that your child will have to continue taking them for as long as they expect to experience relief, potentially for the rest of their life.

As a parent, you can choose whether or not your child takes medication. We recommend making an informed decision based on your options, personal research, and the professional guidance of a licensed medical professional.

Types of ADHD Medication

You now have a realistic perspective on the advantages and disadvantages associated with ADHD medication, but what types of medication are there? There are quite a few options for ADHD medication that can be divided into two groups: stimulant and non-stimulant.

Perhaps the most popular ADHD medication is Adderall; it is the one that you think about when someone mentions ADHD medication, so it might also be the one you are most familiar with. Adderall and similar medications are considered to be stimulant medications due to their effect on dopamine and norepinephrine. ADHD stimulants come in immediate-release formulas that last four to six hours, while extended-release medications offer relief for up to twelve hours.

Some parents shy away from stimulant medicines because of the effects they may have, instead opting for non-stimulant medications. Usually, selective serotonin reuptake inhibitors (SSRIs) are the primary non-stimulant medication prescribed. They work to improve serotonin and

Myth: Medications like Adderall can cure ADHD.

Reality: There is no cure for ADHD. As mentioned, it is a lifelong condition. However, medication has dramatically improved symptoms and enabled children and adults alike to function with ADHD.

other neurotransmitters that empower your child to feel better and focus better. If your child responds poorly to specific medicines, some such as atomoxetine are available as an alternative. Additionally, clonidine alongside stimulants will help treat symptoms like anxiety.

Choosing and Monitoring ADHD Medication

There are a lot of factors involved in the selection and personalization of ADHD medication to suit your child's needs. Understanding such factors will empower you to make wise decisions regarding your child's medication plan and management. Some factors to consider are:

- **Choosing proper medication**: Picking the right medication for your child's needs depends on which symptoms impact them the most, their medical history, and their responses to various medications. A healthcare professional will better be able to guide you in this respect.

- **Dosage and timing**: Monitoring medication and its efficacy involves dosage and timing best practices. Doctors determine dosage based on weight, age, and response to the medication. Medication should be administered at the same time daily for consistency. For example, stimulants would probably best be administered in the mornings to avoid affecting your child's sleep.

- **Monitoring effectiveness**: Schedule regular follow-up appointments to monitor the medication's effectiveness and adjust the dosage if necessary. Observe changes in your child's behavior, academic performance, and overall functioning to see if medication changes are needed.

- **Side effects**: Report any side effects as you see them, as they may indicate a need for a medication change.

- **Combined approach**: Combining medication with other techniques such as behavioral therapy, can also improve your child's medication effectiveness.

It is crucial to collaborate closely with healthcare professionals, communicate openly about your child's response to medication, and actively participate in the monitoring process to ensure the best outcomes for your child and their health.

Common Therapies Used for ADHD:

CBT and DBT

Cognitive Behavioral Therapy is a popular intervention for several mental health concerns and behavioral issues, including ADHD. Primarily, CBT examines how thoughts influence emotions and behavior. This method uses cognitive restructuring, behavioral activation, and exposure to help challenge behavioral patterns and safely modify them.

Many children with ADHD suffer from frustration or low self-esteem because of social stereotypes, challenges in focus, and struggles pertaining to completing tasks. Through cognitive restructuring, CBT can help address negative thought patterns by encouraging your child to recognize these patterns and improve their thinking to become more positive, realistic, and beneficial.

Additionally, CBT focuses strongly on skill-building, especially practical skills teaching organizational and time management skills, for instance. Children who struggle with planning, time awareness, completing tasks, emotional management, and more can benefit from CBT.

> Current research proposes that CBT and DBT should not be stand-alone treatment methods for ADHD. Behavioral interventions work best *in-the-moment*, correcting behaviors as they occur.

CBT works by what is called *behavioral activation*. Examples are encouraging a child to engage in more positive and rewarding activities that improve behavioral management, interacting with others, and their internal emotional state. As a result, a child who undergoes this form of therapy will be more equipped to handle life's challenges, improve their self-esteem, their relationships, and their success at school.

Alternately, **Dialectical Behavioral Therapy** (DBT) emphasizes emotional regulation, pioneering the movement of therapeutic interventions for those with intense and difficult-to-control emotions. It incorporates dialectics, the idea that seemingly opposing ideas can be integrated, such as balancing acceptance and change. Through this type of therapy, your child will practice mindfulness skills, distress tolerance skills, and interpersonal guidance for improved communication. Initially developed to treat borderline personality disorder, DBT has proven its prowess in treating a myriad of conditions.

For ADHD, in particular, DBT can be empowering for children who struggle with emotional regulation. Your child can learn to both identify and manage these intense emotions. It also encourages interpersonal effectiveness. This means DBT can help your child form relationships and communicate easier than ever.

Supplemental Treatments:

Occupational Therapy

Occupational therapy involves helping patients develop, improve, or maintain the skills needed for daily living and overall well-being. Occupational therapists work with people of all ages to address physical, cognitive, sensory, and emotional challenges that may impact their ability to participate in activities and routines. Just a few ways occupational therapy can help include emotional regulation, communication skills, fine and gross motor skills, attention skills, and sensory processing.

While there is no specific therapy for sensory-seeking behaviors, understanding what they are is key to helping your child learn to manage them. Sensory seeking refers to a tendency to seek out sensory stimulation to regulate arousal levels. Children who have difficulties with sensory processing might engage in behaviors aimed at increasing sensory input to feel more alert and focused.

Sensory-seeking behaviors may confuse you as a parent, but to them, it is a crucial part of helping them feel more normal. You must feed their sensory appetite to improve your child's ability to regulate their attention through allowing opportunities for physical activity. Encourage your child to exercise, even if it interrupts their focus. You can also help them sustain focus by offering fidget toys, like spinners and stress balls.

In addition, it is a good idea to include vestibular input into their routine to feed their sensory needs. Vestibular input involves movement that changes the direction of the head, which is quite comforting for kids with ADHD. You might see your child seeking vestibular input by rocking, spinning, or swinging around their limbs. Rather than discourage these behaviors, understand that it is a common sensory input your child needs to regulate themselves. One way to encourage this is by purchasing an exercise ball that they can bounce on when they should be focusing. A trampoline is another tool to help with proprioceptive feedback.

Tactile experiences can help your child with safe and meaningful sensory input. They can also benefit from playing with various textures, such as messy items like finger painting and clay. This type of play can also discourage impulses to feed senses in inappropriate settings, thus improving your child's emotional regulation.

Like most children, kids with ADHD are also prone to putting random objects into their mouths, which is both unsanitary and a choking hazard. Chewable stimulation toys like age-appropriate chewable necklaces and items can be helpful, as can encouraging activities like bubble blowing, crunchy foods, and chewing gum.

Sensory- challenges are not just what you *should* do; but, there are also a few key experiences to avoid: Be mindful of bright lights, loud noises, crowded spaces, and cluttered environments. Some children can become overstimulated and dysregulated.

Mindfulness-Based Exercises

Mindfulness-based interventions involve practices that cultivate awareness, attention, and present-moment focus. These techniques can be beneficial for children with ADHD in promoting self-regulation and reducing impulsivity. Practicing mindfulness exercises alongside your child can be effectively set the stage for their own successful routines. Some mindfulness exercises include:

- **Mindful breathing**: Sit comfortably with your eyes closed. Inhale slowly through the nose, counting to four, and exhale through the mouth for a count of four. Focus on the breath and repeat.
- **Body scan**: Lie down or sit comfortably. Bring attention to different body parts, starting from toes to head, noticing sensations.
- **Progressive muscle relaxation**: Tense and then relax different muscle groups one at a time. Start with the toes and work up to the head, promoting relaxation and body awareness.
- **Guided imagery**: Guide your child through a calming mental journey. Imagine floating on a cloud or exploring a peaceful forest. Encourage detailed visualization.
- **Mindful listening**: Listen attentively to a sound, whether a bell, chimes, or nature sounds. Focus on the sound without trying to label or analyze it.
- **Five senses exercise**: Notice five things you can see, four you can touch, three you can hear, two you can smell, and one thing you can taste.

Guide your child through some of the provided exercises, and discover what they favor and prioritizing those exercises. Introduce mindfulness activities gradually but consistently so they become comfortable with using them in their daily routine.

Lifestyle Changes

Treating ADHD does not only hinge on therapy and medication; there are also simple lifestyle changes that can improve your child's symptoms, such as changes to physical activity, sleep, nutrition, and more.

Physical Activity

Most kids do not get enough physical activity, which can be especially detrimental for a child with ADHD, considering that activities like sports, biking, swimming, and outdoor play can release excess energy and improve focus. Encourage your child to get at least an hour a day of physical activity, but that hour does not have to be consecutive. Some studies have found that at least 15 minutes of intense exercise in the morning can have close to, if not the same, effect as taking ADHD medication.

Quality Sleep

Sleep deprivation is known to exacerbate the symptoms of ADHD, especially for kids. To counteract this, you must help your child get quality rest by creating a soothing bedtime environment and establishing a bedtime routine that allows their mind and body to wind down. Additionally, if your child is taking stimulant medication, it is essential to keep their final dose of the day distanced from bedtime, if possible, as stimulants can cause insomnia.

Screen Time Management

Children with ADHD are known for spending copious amounts of time behind the screen, even more so than neurotypical children. While screen time can be a valuable part of the sensory experience for a neurodiverse child, parents should limit purely recreational screen time to an hour or less per day due to some of the adverse effects it can have. Encourage engaging and educational activities such as puzzles, word games, reading, and role-playing while limiting non-educational screen time.

Healthy Food Rules

What your child eats matters, as the foods that they eat can also significantly impact the severity of their ADHD-related symptoms. Some fundamental rules include getting high-quality calories, adequate hydration, lean protein, smart carbohydrates, and healthy fats. It is always wise to avoid feeding children too many foods with sugar and processed foods, which include additional additives and preservatives. Such ingredients can exacerbate the symptoms of ADHD, so we recommend paying attention to what your child eats and the resulting reaction to identify foods your child may be particularly sensitive to.

While incorporating all these lifestyle changes at once might seem overwhelming, incorporating some slowly and over time can have significant benefits.

The Importance of Consistency in Treatment

In the last section, we discussed the value of consistency in medication management. Still, the importance of consistency extends to all areas of ADHD treatment, especially for children. Consistency is the fastest and most effective way to promote long-term positive outcomes in the course of their treatment.

Tips for consistency with your child's treatment

- Maintain consistent daily routines for waking up, meals, homework, and bedtime.
- Use visual schedules and reminders to reinforce routines.
- Set specific times for medication.
- Schedule regular follow-up appointments with healthcare professionals to monitor treatment effectiveness.
- Collaborate with teachers to maintain consistency in interventions across different environments.
- Involve your child in decision-making regarding their treatment.
- Reinforce positive behaviors through consistent praise and rewards.
- Educate family members, teachers, and peers about the value of consistent support.
- Ensure that caregivers have adequate support and self-care practices.
- Be flexible with strategies based on your child's changing needs.
- Regularly reassess and adjust treatment plans in collaboration with healthcare professionals.

Key Takeaways from this Chapter

The main points we want you to leave this chapter knowing are:

1. Meeting a child's basic needs is vital to help control symptoms and behaviors associated with ADHD. A sleep-deprived or malnourished child cannot function better, no matter how many skills they learn.

2. ADHD treatments can be highly successful in helping to build a child's executive function skills and curbing symptoms that can result in unwanted behavior. However, no treatment is a cure; many treatments have their pros and cons, and are best when combined with other treatment options.

3. The most common ADHD treatments are Behavioral Parent Training (BPT), medication (stimulant and non-stimulant), and therapies such as Cognitive Behavioral Therapy (CBT) and Dialectical Behavioral Therapy (DBT).

4. Better lifestyle choices and consistency in treatment are two fundamental techniques to ensuring success in building your child's functioning skills.

ACTIVITY: Building Your Child's Care Plan

Regardless of your child's symptoms, they will need you to establish a care plan for them. Building a care plan involves researching, reaching out, and finding options available to you and your child for support.

Now that you know some treatment options, take the time to research them further and identify what you think may help your child. Use the form like the example below to record the advantages and disadvantages. Consider factors such as the availability, cost, insurance coverage possibilities, how much of your time it will require, and how long it will take to begin the treatment.

Research providers in your area to see which will best suit your family. There is no requirement to make a commitment now or to use any of these treatment options. Our aim is to introduce you to what may be available to you and your child.

Example ADHD Child Treatment Plan

ADHD Child Treatment Plan			
Treatments: Which methods do I/we think are best suited to our child (e.g. BPT, medication, OT, others)?	1.	2.	3.
For each method listed above, we've researched options and have considered these factors:			
Pros:	1.	2.	3.
Cons:	1.	2.	3.
Cost:	1.	2.	3.
Availability:	1.	2.	3.
Insurance coverage:	1.	2.	3.

Chapter 3 – Your Role as a Parent of a Child with ADHD

"Parent the child you have, not the child you wish you had."

—Unknown

L et's face it: not many of us were prepared for parenthood. It is not like we were trained in what to do in most situations. We all strive to be good parents, but the sad fact is that many parents try to parent a child they expected to have rather than the one sitting in front of them.

Parenting children with ADHD is almost common-sense good parenting. If you also have neurotypical children, consider how many times you've helped that child memorize facts for a test, take turns when playing games, get ready for school, or walk through the steps to clean their room. Have you ever made checklists to remind them of the order in which steps must be completed? How about teaching your child how to make good decisions, control their emotions, or keep track of their belongings? If you answered yes to any of this, you already understand what it takes to be a good parent. You already have some excellent parenting skills under your belt.

Keep in mind that as your child grows, you will need to tweak these strategies to be age-appropriate. And one last word: do not expect immediate results, much less perfection. You will most likely see slight decreases in undesirable and positive behavior. Stay consistent with their treatment plan. As mentioned, ADHD is NOT just something that kids grow out of. Although their struggles will lessen as they reach adulthood, they will discover they must fall back on the skills you've taught them. Your job is to ensure they have the tools in their toolbox for when their inattention, hyperactivity, or impulsiveness manifests.

The Importance of Positive Parent-Child Relationships

A positive parent-child relationship is instrumental to your child's success and your connection with them. Benefits of a positive parent-child relationship include:

- **Creating a nurturing environment**: When you serve as a positive figure for your child, they will feel more nurtured and supported. This nurturing environment allows your child to flourish and feel cared for—and enhances your personal bond.
- **Enhancing communication and emotional development**: When you serve as a positive figure in your child's life, they learn communication and emotional intelligence-related skills pertaining to their future needs.
- **Improving trust and security**: A strong relationship between parent and child will empower your child to trust you and feel secure within your care.
- **Encouraging positive behavior**: A good relationship posits you as a role model *and* authority figure. This will encourage your child to listen, respect, and admire you, all while engaging in positive behaviors from a place of genuine consideration.

When you have a strong bond with your child, you feel loved, supported, and appreciated. You also have a firm understanding of their needs, empowering you to be a more supportive parent. So, what can you do to incentivize and strengthen trust and closeness in your parent-child relationship?

Declarative Language vs. Commands

I once overheard a person say, "We spend the first couple years of our children's lives telling them to walk and talk and the rest of their childhood telling them to sit down and be quiet." As amusing as that may be, the reality is that the parent is the problem in that scenario, not the child. We spend our lives bossing our kids around while they ultimately learn to ignore and sometimes even rebel against that approach.

Declarative language is stating a situation out loud instead of issuing commands to get your child to perform something. It is a common parenting practice you already use. Maybe you have said something out loud about whether you liked a song, felt a specific emotion when you saw someone you love, or weren't sure how to decide between two choices for lunch. The objective of declarative language is to teach your child how to interpret your intent and choose to act on it.

Examples of Using Declarative Language	
Instead of saying:	Try saying:
Put your coat on	Brrrr, it looks cold outside. I think it would feel warmer with a coat on.
Go wash your hands	I notice your hands look dirty.
Hang up your backpack	I can see that your backpack is on the floor.
Look at me when I talk to you	I feel like you are not listening when you don't look at me.
Get your shoes on	It is almost time to leave; I wonder where your shoes are.
Clean up your room	I see there is so much stuff on your floor.

Issuing commands, also called using *imperative language*, doesn't always work is because it tends to put a person on the defensive side. There is a right or wrong answer to the question, and people get nervous that they may pick the wrong one. The opposite is true of declarative language, which can foster a sense of cooperation. It provides an opportunity for independent thinking and problem-solving.

For example, when the dog barks to go outside, instead of commanding your child to "Go let the dog out," try observing the situation out loud: "Hmm… it sounds like the dog needs to go outside." Instead of directing them to "Get ready for school," say, "It is almost time to leave for school." Instead of telling them to "Say you are sorry," try telling them, "Aww, your brother looks sad now. He might need a hug." Here are some basic examples and general tips for using declarative language.

Try to practice saying your observations out loud, and avoid using your child's name or the word "you" in the statement if you can. Instead, try to use "I," "we," or "us" pronouns with verbs that describe our thinking process. Doing this will strengthen your child's executive functioning skills by echoing your thinking pattern while observing you draw conclusions and plan how to respond without the defensive feeling that they're being told to do something.

Communicate Clearly and Be Specific

There is a time and place for declarative language—it is excellent for teaching your child problem-solving and independent thinking. But if your child is in danger and must follow your instructions, you should not use declarative language. In that case, it is more important to command them to get out of the street or don't touch that iron because it is hot.

But sometimes, clear communication is vital when teaching a child how to follow instructions. Most of the time, children with ADHD need more clarity than "Go get ready for bed." Let's be honest: if you are vague, you have no idea what your child will do, and they have yet to learn what you expect. Therefore, you may need to break down the steps you want them to perform.

Another practice that should be common sense, but is rarely performed these days, is ensuring you have your child's attention and not just *barking orders* from across the room. Instead, go to where they are and establish eye contact. Do NOT compete with the iPad when giving directions—you will only be frustrating yourself. If you don't ensure you have their complete attention, you will find yourself having to repeat what you're saying, probably more than once. Although, It will help to have them repeat your instructions so you know they heard you correctly. Then, ask if they have any questions before they begin, giving you the chance to correct their understanding of what is expected.

Connection Time

If your kids are in elementary school, they have probably heard about bucket filling. As a school counselor, I taught students that how we treat a person is either going to fill their bucket (make them feel good) or dip from their bucket (make them feel bad). It is a simple analogy I used to show how our actions influence those around us. Connection time is an excellent tool that doesn't take much time or effort, but its effects can last for a long time. You are filling your child's bucket daily, which will, in turn, produce more positive behaviors.

When my children were little, I stayed home to raise them. I would get up in the morning to get started on my day (after coffee and random scrolling on my phone, of course). However, I knew the day would go smoother if I took about twenty minutes to play with my daughter, doing what she wanted. I found out early on that when I took time to have a connection time like this first thing in the morning, she was happier and more cooperative thru the rest of the day. She started bringing up things she was struggling with, and began to look forward to this special time with me every day. I learned so much about her that I may not have if we did not share this time together.

Connection time can be done any time of the day; it just needs to be a set period for which you give your child undivided attention. Regardless of the time of day, the key is to encourage them to pick activities that they enjoy so that you can share their interests. This might be playing dolls, reading a book, playing a board game, shooting baskets, or allowing them to tell you about their favorite cartoon characters.

If you stay dedicated to doing this, it can continue into middle school or until your child no longer wants to do it. But whatever you end up doing for connection time, don't go in with the idea that you should be teaching lessons during this time or that it allows you to pry into their lives. The objective here is to allow them to take the lead in your time together and to let them be themselves without critique or criticism. Consistency and dedication to this special time together build your child's trust in you and consequently strengthen your bond.

Practice Reflective Listening

Your child's words can provide insight into their interests, values, and feelings. Practice actively listening by stopping what you are doing and giving them your undivided attention as soon as possible. Then, reflect those words and emotions back to them. Our daughter used tell me I was wrong about what was upsetting her. It took time for to realize I needed to pause and allow her to talk, then repeat back what I thought she way saying or feeling.

Also, ask questions and share their interests. Let them know you are paying attention and they are being heard. The benefit of demonstrating reflective listening is that they pick this skill up and will develop better relationships with others.

Setting Boundaries

As parents, we tend to do almost everything for our kids when we become anxious or overwhelmed. Doing this blurs the line of where your role as a parent ends and your child's begins. Of course we want to guide, mentor, and nurture them. But sometimes, we over-share with our children about our lives or we live through them vicariously. Sometimes we even allow them to cause us to fall apart when they throw a tantrum instead of being firm and modeling proper emotional self-regulation ourselves. Instead, we can eliminate the power struggle preventing your child from baiting you into arguments or partake in yelling matches. Being scared of losing your relationship with your child is not an excuse to give in to tantrums. It needs to be clearly established who is in control.

Children feel safer when they know parents are in charge. It can be scary to hold too much power as a young child. When we mention allowing your child to lead during playtime or giving them autonomy and independence, we are not saying give up any of your parental authority or allow them to interfere with your personal relationships. You must establish clear boundaries of what your child can and can't do regarding your privacy, personal space, and that of other family members.

Recognizing and Nurturing Your Child's Unique Strengths

Some people believe that children with ADHD have few talents or skills. After all, ADHD is much like a disability in many ways. They obviously don't recognize that children with ADHD can have many strengths. Therefore, it is crucial to discover and encourage your child's unique strengths to help you nurture those talents and skills.

We've talked about children with ADHD having a fantastic ability to hyperfocus on something they feel passionately about. They also tend to have extreme imaginations and endless creativity—they think in novel and innovative ways. Many of today's leading industries look for people who think outside the box, those with a knack for creative problem-solving and finding unique solutions that most overlook.

Also, kids with ADHD typically have no problem with enthusiasm, impulsivity, and spontaneity. To their friends, it is what makes them fun to be around, and definitely what gives them such uplifting dispositions. This freeing personality and positive mindset can contribute to more genuine relationships and better mental health. Although having ADHD is challenging, kids who learn to thrive with their condition tend to be more resilient, meaning they can bounce back from life's setbacks and more readily handle adversity.

A significant focus of your parenting will be learning to empower your child to hone their skills and use their natural talents to their advantage. The objective should be overall growth and progress because a person's skills, traits, and values do not remain constant throughout their lives. We should strive to help our children understand that they have the power to grow, change, and improve.

Celebrating Success and Fostering a Positive Self-Image

All children should be recognized for accomplishments because it boosts their confidence and give them an extra push to continue making improvements. Celebrating successes helps them foster a positive self-image. Many children who have ADHD struggle with self-image more than children without it, so helping your child bolster their self-image is powerful for them.

Recognize When They Are Doing Good

It is easy to reprimand a child for undesirable behavior, but we overlook when they do well or make good choices. For example, imagine you are running late and trying to get out the door quickly, but you notice your child doesn't have their coat on. So, you might ask them, "Why aren't you ready to go? I told you we need to leave." However, instead of reprimanding them for not taking all the necessary steps to get ready, you should comment on the steps they performed successfully. Did they already put their shoes on, but maybe they need their coat or backpack? Perhaps they forgot to use the bathroom? Try praising them for accomplishing the things they did do, and add a gentle reminder of what still needs to be done. It could go something like: "Great job putting your shoes on and grabbing your backpack! Now, we just need you to put your coat on, and we will be ready to leave."

Another way to recognize them when they are doing well is to create a situation where the child can prove they've learned something you are working with them on. For example, if you are working on sharing with a sibling, create a situation where your child has to share.

Notice any steps they are making towards sharing and praise them for taking those steps, even if they don't meet expectations.

My daughter always wanted to be first in line and also did not like sharing with her brother. It often ended with her hitting him or throwing something. One day, during our nightly connection time, she told me she felt like a bad person. She gets yelled at for everything and doesn't do anything good. That confession was a wake-up call for me. So, I started praising her every time I noticed her trying to stay calm by pausing or taking a breath before reacting. I practiced catching it in the moment and ensuring she knew I saw her staying calm and that I was proud of her.

Her favorite treat at the time was bubble gum. We had a small toy gumball machine, so I'd give her a coin to get a gumball out whenever I caught her pausing to think before she acted. Over time, she actually learned to pause when she did not get her way instead of lashing out. Try to implement catching your child in the moment when they are working on their skills at home, at the playground, everywhere else.

Another idea that parents and teachers can use is notes of positive praise. When you catch your child *in-the-moment* working on behavior or improving a trouble area, you can also write a praise for them on a notepad or create a little chart to give them to say, "Hey, I noticed you being kind today," or "I noticed you brought everything you needed to class today." A simple, written note of positive praise can go a long way to encouraging them.

Parent Self-Care Strategies

Ok, parents, we must talk about one of the most critical ways you can help your child: by taking care of yourself first. It can be challenging to find the available space for self-care in your busy life. But you have to realize that you cannot make impactful changes in your children's lives if you do not get the basic attention your body and mind need as well, such as:

- Quality sleep and general physical rest
- Taking the opportunity to decompress (mental rest)
- Stepping away from emotionally draining situations
- Regular exercise promotes a healthy cardiovascular system
- Proper nutrition to ensure you are getting all the right vitamins and nutrients
- Taking your medication as directed
- Having time for relationships outside of your parenting responsibilities

Personal self-care goes a long way to ensuring you are in good health and are present for your children. As with many areas of life, the key is to make small but impactful changes rather than attempting to change everything at once to provide a feeling of accomplishment. You must connect with your mind, body, and soul in ways that ensure your health and well-being.

Even if the concept of taking time for yourself makes you feel guilty, you must make it a priority. You cannot remain patient and calm if you are sleep-deprived or at the end of your rope. You will overreact and then feel guilty later. Self-care really isn't an option; it is vital for effectively parenting a child with ADHD.

Remember, don't just say you will take better care of yourself—create a plan. Put activities on your calendar that will benefit you like going to the gym, reading a book, getting a message, etc. Get childcare if necessary to make it happen! Otherwise, you will neglect your needs which will ultimately affect your relationships and your competence in helping your children.

Stay Calm and Stop Yelling

Even if you do your best to ensure that your child's energy is balanced, you may still encounter exhaustion, depression, emotional distancing, shame, and more. But you must realize that a child with ADHD will experience developmental delays compared to non-

ADHD kids. Their overall maturity level will be two, maybe three years behind their peers, which will be overwhelming and can make it hard to remain calm and consistent in your parenting techniques.

The exciting thing is that the same routines you establish for your child will benefit you as well. When you know what to expect each day, you are more likely to feel comfortable with what comes next. It is easy to give in to avoid a meltdown and keep the peace. Stil, in the long run, this is detrimental to the overall objective of teaching your child behavior management and emotional self-regulation.

A good rule of thumb is to pick your battles. Do not make every situation a big deal. Breaking minor rules doesn't require immediate intervention, nor does a setback equal failure. Remember, it is more important to choose the most impactful behaviors to work on because you won't be able to change everything overnight. Manage your expectations, pick your battles, and focus on celebrating small victories along the way. Progress will be gradual — recognizing that will be crucial.

The Value of Strong Support Networks and How to Find Them

Your role as a parent is complicated—ADHD only adds to the traditional challenges of parenting, highlighting the importance of something crucial: a strong support network. Support networks are invaluable resources for meeting others like you which gives you the opportunity to see what others are going through and talk to them about their strategies. This can also be a great way to get resource referrals from parents who have met success by using specific resources or treatments.

We recommend looking into some already established ADHD-related support networks. Some good options include the Attention Deficit Disorder Association (ADDA), Children and Adults with Attention-Deficit/Hyperactivity Disorder (CHADD), and ADDitude magazine's contact options. Some of these sites have an ADHD Helpline or contact information to reach out to when you feel like you have no other options. They can help you find resources in your community to connect you with others.

Key Takeaways from this Chapter

The main points we want you to leave this chapter knowing are:

1. Parenting a child with ADHD begins with positive parenting—your relationship with your child is crucial for their development.

2. The way you talk to a child with ADHD is significant—use declarative language instead of yelling commands from across the room.

3. Be clear with your instructions when helping them learn a skill. Being vague confuses a child, and now neither of you knows what to expect next.

4. Please connect with your child individually for at least 15 minutes a day to keep their *bucket* full. Remember, this is *their* time.

5. Listening, showing respect, and setting boundaries are essential for a parent to establish trust with their child.

6. Celebrate their strengths and recognize when they are improving. It means the world to them.

7. Just as important is taking care of yourself. Don't let the stress of raising a neurodiverse child keep you from meeting your needs, too!

ACTIVITY: Practicing Declarative Language

Throughout your day, pay close attention to the language you use when you interact with your child. If you can pause before giving commands, or if you can remember right after issuing one, try to think of ways to rephrase it using declarative language instead. If you need examples, refer to the chart we provided earlier in this chapter.

Additionally, notice how your child responds to both issuing commands and using declarative statements. Did you see a difference? After a while, you should notice them pausing to think about what you just said. If you are doing it correctly, you will be making observations out loud that will enable your child to make decisions about how they act based on your observation.

Give this a couple of weeks and see how your child behaves. Do they comply more easily with declarative statements? Did their behavior change at all?

Chapter 4 – Strategies for Building Executive Functioning Skills

"Executive function has nothing to do with intelligence. It has everything to do with how well you can access and demonstrate your intellectual potential." —Tera Sumpter, Seeds of Learning

Earlier, we introduced executive function and how ADHD can impair our ability to self-manage our emotions and behavior. These skills develop as we grow and improve as we become adults. Since we know that children with ADHD are typically two to three years behind their peers in maturity, this helps us understand why we must support our children in ways that develop these skills.

A study in which researchers trained children with ADHD and coached their parents in developing executive functioning skills resulted in these children performing virtually as well as other children at similar ages. These results demonstrate that parent intervention focusing on improving executive function skills can effectively address skill deficiencies where medication and talk therapy cannot.

There are many tools at our disposal to help our children develop executive function. Remember, when a child gets good sleep, regular exercise, proper nutrition, and adequate hydration, they will be more successful in self-managing these areas of their lives. If parents work diligently at building daily routines and habits for them, there will be noticeable differences in their skill levels in even a short period of time.

When examining executive functioning skills, many theories and models are available to understand how the brain helps us manage ourselves. Just search the Internet for executive functioning, and you will see varying lists of three, seven, ten, twelve, and more—and the lists will not always agree or contain the same skills. That's ok! The purpose here isn't to align with any given model or theory. We want to expose you to a set of skills that experts feel apply to children with ADHD, and to provide you with an understanding of what normally developed executive functioning skills should look like and how to create those in your child.

ADHD and Developmental Delays in Executive Function	
Chronological Age	Executive Function Age
5	3-1/2
6	4
7	5
8	5-1/2
9	6
10	7
11	8
12	8-1/2

The key to avoiding overwhelm is to focus on only one behavior at a time. Prioritize just the one or two behaviors that seem to be the most troublesome for your child, or family, and it becomes more manageable than trying to tackle all behaviors at once.

But don't get discouraged if situations get worse before they get better. Sometimes, it happens, and you should be ready for new behaviors or adverse reactions to these new parenting techniques. Be patient, give the strategies time to work, and watch how your child strives to show progress. Improving your child's executive function will be a learning process for both of you, but it pays off significantly when you've established sound positive reinforcement and improved your relationship.

On the following pages in this chapter, we've developed charts showing common executive functioning skills and some tools and strategies you can use to help improve these in your child. The next section aims to be a reference guide for when you are working on a problematic behavior or need help choosing the steps to use. You can bookmark specific ones you are working on and flip back to that strategy as required.

Look back at the ABC Chart you created. Consider which area of executive function impacts your child's behavior in those situations. Then, identify the tools below that you can implement to help them improve that behavior.

Attention Control

- What does this skill look like once developed?
  - Ignoring distractions
  - Refocusing when distractions occur

Tools and Strategies to Improve

- Exercise with your kid regularly, preferably first thing in the morning. Take them on a 30-minute walk, to a playground or park, or teach them isometric exercises and do it with them for 20-30 minutes.
- Teach them to plan the activity ahead of time so they know the purpose and duration of the task (more on Time Management later).
- Teach them how to break tasks into manageable chunks to avoid overwhelm, such as 15-minute intervals with a 5-minute break.
- Teach them to recognize when they are bored or frustrated and take breaks when that occurs.
- Teach them how to eliminate distractions from their workspace by placing those items out of reach or in another room. If other children in class are distracting them, ask the teacher if they can sit in the front of the room.
- Teach them how to ignore distractions when they arise. Sometimes, giving them a fidget toy or other sensory gadget can help them focus.

Emotional Self-Regulation

- What does this skill look like once developed?
  - Self-managing the intensity of one's emotions.
  - Reacting in a positive manner that doesn't harm others.
  - Not losing control when one experiences triggers.

Tools and Strategies to Improve

- Teach your child to notice how they feel when they get upset. For example, do they feel their heart speed up? Do they notice their stomach getting upset? Do they feel parts of their body tense up?
- Teach them to identify triggers that make them mad or sad and how to expect and accept what emotion will follow.
- Teach your child to engage in self-talk and name what they feel. Model this behavior: "I have so much to do, I feel overwhelmed and anxious."
- Teach them to pause and think when they get mad, sad, excited, scared, embarrassed, etc., and make a choice about how they will respond.
- Establish a place in the home where they can go when upset. Give them activities to do or teach mindfulness exercises to calm down.
- Help them create a list of coping activities for when they are bored, disappointed, sad, angry, etc.

Cognitive Flexibility

- What does this skill look like once developed?
    - Being able to deal with change.
    - Accepting when things don't go your way.
    - Being able to switch between tasks when they change.

Tools and Strategies to Improve

- Teach your child how to notice when change makes them upset and when not getting their way triggers a response.

- If you notice them complaining or getting bored with their routine, switch it up a bit so it differs slightly each day and see how they respond.

- Teach them to pause and think when they don't get their way and to consider how it makes them feel or how it could be a positive thing.

- Teach them to use problem-solving when life doesn't go their way. Having a backup plan is an essential skill everyone should learn in life.

- Play "random day" with everyone making random decisions. Teach them to be creative with their decisions and flexible with others'.

- Teach them to rephrase when they are not understood and to ask for a "free pass" or "do-over" when they say something without thinning.

- Teach them patience when a game glitches, an app crashes, a belonging breaks, or they lose something important.

Impulse Control

- What does this skill look like once developed?
  - Also called response inhibition or self-restraint, it is the suppression of inappropriate actions in response to triggers or distractions.
  - Being able to resist temptation (exercise delayed gratification).
  - To resist doing something that seems fun but may hurt others.

Tools and Strategies to Improve

- Establish household rules and teach your child why each rule is important, then practice praising them in the moment for when they follow the rules.
- Teach them self-talk and model it so they see you resisting the urge to do something, and explain to them how you are making that decision.
- Teach them how to pause and consider making good decisions about responding. You could use a visual timer to count down.
- Teach them to use problem-solving skills when things don't go their way, so they do not feel the urge to steal, lie, or destroy someone else's belongings because they don't have them.
- Teach them anger management skills like breathing techniques and how to use them when their emotions are high.
- Play games with them that teach impulse control, such as "Red Light-Green Light" and "Follow the Leader."

Metacognition / Self-Awareness

- What does this skill look like once developed?
  - Being self-aware and aware of our surroundings.
  - Reflecting on our thoughts and making decisions or solving problems based on those thoughts.

Tools and Strategies to Improve

- Teach your child to think out loud and model it for them so they see and hear you making decisions.
- Reduce negative self-talk in the household so that they learn to be positive by hearing you making positive comments about yourself or others.
- Use reflective questioning with your child so they have to pause and think about their thoughts and feelings before they answer.
- Teach them to compare and contrast by describing things they enjoy.
- Use declarative language instead of imperative language so there is no immediate right or wrong answer; instead, it is an open-ended one.
- Ask them questions emphasizing processes and solutions, such as "How will you know when you are finished?" or "How could you have handled this differently?"
- Teach them to take notes about how they feel and what they observe when on outings or at the end of the day.

Organization

- What does this skill look like once developed?
  - Putting things where they belong and cleaning up after ourselves.
  - Using systematic orders for items such as alphabetical or sequential
  - Collecting, categorizing, and repeating structured information.

Tools and Strategies to Improve

- Teach your child structure and create a consistent and predictable daily routine so they can keep their schedule organized throughout the day.
- Teach them to keep items in a specific place by color-coding, putting numbers on storage bins, or labeling shelves.
- Help them remember to stay organized by using declarative language and open-ended questions to help them think about where they have put things or where items belong.
- Teach time management so they can estimate how long tasks take and learn to fit activities in when they have the proper amount of time.
- Create visual cues/checklists so they can walk through the steps in order.
- Consider purchasing a daily planner that they can use to keep track of assignments, deadlines, and activities.
- Teach them to chunk activities into manageable pieces, such as 15 minutes with a 5-minute break, to avoid getting overwhelmed.

Planning and Prioritization

- What does this skill look like once developed?

  o The ability to create a strategy before starting an activity to achieve a specific objective.

  o Sometimes, it is regarded as thinking about future activities and planning accordingly, such as To-Do Lists.

  o Remembering to bring essential tools or materials to accomplish tasks.

Tools and Strategies to Improve

- Begin by creating a consistent and predictable daily routine so your child knows what to expect every day. Walk through the routine with them often so they learn the order of steps they are to complete.

- Teach your child how to follow steps in an activity and perform them in the correct sequence by using visuals such as charts and checklists.

- Teach them to create a list of steps to complete an activity so they can determine what step should be performed in what order.

- Teach reverse planning of a task so they can examine all the steps required, where they go, in what order, and how long each step takes.

- Model planning by practicing thinking out loud so they can hear and see you planning steps to accomplish something.

- Help them understand time management, schedules, calendars, and clocks and how these fit into everything they do.

Task Initiation / Completion

- What does this skill look like once developed?
    - Beginning a task or activity when needed without expecting reminders from someone else to begin.
    - Avoiding distractions, wasting time, delaying starting a task, and general procrastination.
    - Following directions and fully engaging in a task.

Tools and Strategies to Improve

- Teach your child to perform steps in the order expected without reminders by using visual cues, charts, and checklists for them to refer to.

- Use alarms, timers, and any method of reminding them when to start a task and gradually decrease the use of these over time.

- Make sure your instructions to them are clear so there is little room for interpretation when teaching them a skill.

- Teach them to chunk activities into manageable pieces to avoid getting overwhelmed, such as 15 minutes with a 5-minute break.

- Teach them how to identify which activities are important and decide when to do something over a preferred activity.

- Have them repeat your instructions after you've given them so you know they understand what is expected of them, giving you the opportunity to clarify what they might not have right.

Time Management

- What does this skill look like once developed?
    - Prioritizing tasks and using time effectively to accomplish them.
    - Completing steps within an appropriate amount of time.
    - Accurately estimate how long a task takes and act accordingly.

Tools and Strategies to Improve

- Create a consistent and predictable daily routine for your child so they learn what to expect and when events occur throughout the day.
- Teach your child to do one thing at a time, set time limits, and focus on blocking out distractions.
- Teach them to follow schedules by creating visual cues, charts, and checklists that they can refer to often.
- Teach them to chunk activities into manageable pieces, such as 15 minutes with a 5-minute break, to avoid becoming overwhelmed.
- Practice prioritizing tasks with them so they understand which are important, which are preferred, and in which order to perform them.
- Teach them how to eliminate distractions from their workspace by placing those items out of reach or in another room. If other children in class are distracting them, ask if they can sit in the front of the room.
- Practice talking out loud and teach them self-talk so they can hear and see you performing time management and can follow your lead.

Working Memory

- What does this skill look like once developed?
    - Being able to hold information in the brain and recall details.
    - The ability to create and memorize lists in sequential order.
    - Following multi-step directions to complete tasks and activities.

Tools and Strategies to Improve

- Provide your child with a structured, distraction-free environment to practice following directions and memorizing facts.
- Teach your child to follow schedules by creating visual cues, charts, and checklists that they can refer to often for aid in recalling information.
- Make sure your instructions to them are clear so there is little room for interpretation when teaching them how to follow steps in order.
- Use puzzles and memory games, such as crosswords, pattern recognition, and memory puzzles, to help them strengthen their memory.
- Teach them to make up fictional stories so they learn to remember important details and repeat them to others. Using mnemonic devices such as acrostics is also helpful for remembering names or details.
- Teach them to chunk activities into manageable pieces, such as 15 minutes with a 5-minute break, to avoid getting overwhelmed.

You may notice that we recommend some of the same tools and strategies for developing different executive functioning skills in your child. You may also notice that we believe that some specific interventions you perform will help in multiple areas.

In the upcoming chapters, we will explore a few specific skills we feel are extremely important to focus on, such as behavior mastery, emotional self-regulation, social skills, academic success, and more. We hope that these chapters provide the tools and strategies you require to help you develop these skills in your child.

Key Takeaways from this Chapter

The main points we want you to leave this chapter knowing are:

1. A child with ADHD will typically develop at a rate around 30% slower than their peers, give or take. Keep this in mind as you work with them so you know what to expect when it differs from other kids their age.

2. Keeping track of your child's progress is important to see when it is trending upwards (improving) or if another strategy is needed for them to succeed.

3. Don't get discouraged! Try another strategy and keep your therapist or counselor in the loop so they can suggest adjustments.

Chapter 5 – Strategies for Building a Successful Daily Routine

---

"Success is not final, failure is not fatal: it is the courage to continue that counts."—Winston Churchill

---

H ave you ever felt overwhelmed by the daily challenges of parenting a child with ADHD? You are not alone. You are often unsure what to expect when you try a new technique to manage some dysregulation. One size doesn't fit all—what works for one child won't for the next. It can be frustrating and seem like an uphill battle.

The most impactful changes you can make to your child's life are establishing daily routines, creating visual schedules and cues for them to follow, and creating a structured and distraction-free environment. Although the techniques to achieve this vary, such routines and structure are valuable for any child with ADHD.

When a person consistently follows a routine, it becomes a habit over time. So, the more time you spend building routines with your child, the less time you spend managing behaviors in the long run. In this chapter, we will explore practical strategies that can turn those challenges into opportunities for growth and connection.

Establishing Routines

We want to help you build the routines that will benefit your child in every area of life, building habits and skills to create them. Before we explore creating schedules, let's affirm the benefits consistent routines can provide your child.

What Consistent Routines Provide:

- **Predictability and stability**: Routines provide a sense of predictability and stability in your child's environment. Knowing what to expect helps reduce anxiety and stress, promoting a sense of security.
- **Executive function support**: Children with ADHD often struggle with executive functions like planning, organization, and time management. Routines serve as external organizers, guiding them through tasks and activities.
- **Reduced decision-making stress**: Routines minimize the need for constant decision-making, which can overwhelm children with ADHD. Having set routines eliminates the stress of figuring out what to do next.
- **Improved time management**: Kids with ADHD may struggle with time perception and time management. Routines help structure the day, making it easier for children to transition between activities and meet deadlines.
- **Enhanced focus and attention**: Knowing the sequence of tasks in a routine allows children to shift their attention more smoothly. It reduces the need for constant redirection and improves sustained focus.
- **Established habits**: Routines assist in forming positive habits. By consistently following a set routine, your child can develop habits that contribute to their well-being, such as regular bedtime or homework time.

- **Independence and self-regulation**: Predictable routines empower children with ADHD to become more independent. Knowing what comes next allows them to take initiative and participate in daily activities with greater confidence.

Create a Schedule

Creating your child's schedule should rely primarily on your guidance, but your child should also have input. Let them make some decisions, like what needs to be done and when they do it. For example, you can ask, "When you get home from school, would you rather do your homework right away and have the whole afternoon free, or do you want to have a snack and relax before homework?" Using this method, your child will feel freer to choose tasks without feeling overwhelmed by decisions.

Below are a few options you could include on a daily chart for your child. Since visual cues help with memorizing steps in a routine, you should include a little clipart as a reminder of what that step looks like. Or better yet, you can snap little pictures of your child doing that step and crop them to place on their chart. Either way, giving them the steps with visual cues will be the most effective way of assisting them with developing their daily routines.

A schedule like this can take less than an hour to decide what you and your children must do each day and when you should do it. This schedule will also help your child understand their responsibilities and your expectations, not to mention save you countless hours of repeating yourself and explaining steps over again every day.

My Child's Daily Routine						
Morning						
Use the potty	Eat Breakfast	Brush your teeth	Put PJs in laundry	Get dressed for school	Put on your shoes	Grab Backpack
After School						
Hang up your backpack	Play time	Wash hands for dinner	Dinner time	Help in kitchen	Play time	Pick up toys
Bedtime						
Brush your teeth	Bath time	Put on PJs	Put dirty clothes in laundry	Story time	Lights out	Go to sleep

At first, you will want to keep the schedule light, like the example above, to ease your child into the process and avoid it from seeming overwhelming to them. By creating visual charts like this one, your child can learn what is expected to be done, when, by whom, and how long it should take.

Your child will no doubt need encouragement and additional instruction on each task before this becomes a daily routine and comes even close to being something they will start doing on their own. However, once you have established schedules and your child has lots of practice with this process, it can get to where it is on autopilot. It is possible that your child will develop habits from these routines. Then, you can add more challenging tasks to the schedule to help them grow and build on to the basic tasks, all the while taking on new responsibilities as they get older.

A secret strategy that many behavioral coaches teach is to help your child develop *keystone* habits. This means starting a routine that develops habits that affect two or three other areas of your day. Getting 15 minutes of exercise in the morning every day helps with sleep, eating, attention, learning, etc. These habits act as a catalyst in a chain reaction and can be obvious but not always simple to implement daily. Some examples are creating a morning routine, setting out what you will wear for tomorrow the night before, devoting time to read and meditate, having a family dinner, and journaling, such as keeping track of what you eat or recording what you were most thankful for that day before going to bed. Helping your child create these habits by building them into their daily routines can help increase their self-awareness and self-reflection and assist them with setting goals and seeing them through.

Give Your Child Choices

Giving your child choices for completing an activity can help them accomplish the task(s) and help them feel more agreeable as if they had a part in the task rather than just being told to do it. For example, provide them with a list of activities to complete to practice writing, spelling, or math for them to choose from. This can include using flash math flash cards, using words in a sentence, or writing a short story about something they love using specific words. Make sure you present the list in a visual way. The issue with a child's working memory is that they cannot hold a lot of information in their head at one time. Therefore, visual lists can aid with this.

Pay attention to whether they like being given a choice or if they lock up. When options are open-ended, your child may feel overwhelmed, as if there are too many options to make a good choice. If you notice this, limit the choices to a few. Cover the bottom half of the list and see if this makes it easier for them to decide. If they are worried that their choice will be *the wrong one*, assure them that it can't be wrong; they are choosing what to do next, and there will be plenty of opportunities to make another selection in the future.

Have them circle the choice they made this time to refer back to it when the decision comes up again. They can see you are keeping track and this can help limit the overwhelming feeling of having too many options or making the wrong decision.

Create a Structured Environment

The physical environment of a home or classroom has an effect on your child's ability to pay attention, focus on a given task, and perform well when learning or completing that task. This means your job is to ensure that the specific environment is predictable, organized, and free from distractions, but also that it contains the necessary resources for them to know what to expect and to carry out their routines in this environment. This applies to all children and adults, but especially those with ADHD. Have you ever been in a cluttered room and felt overwhelmed, like there was a lot going on? Or the opposite, where you were in a spacious room and felt calm and focused.

Because children with ADHD are challenged when it comes to structuring their lives due to their lack of ability to self-regulate, they need more external help to be successful. This means by building routines, establishing rules, and proving a structured environment, everyday activities that most kids can do without help can also become routine skills for a child with ADHD too.

Strategies for creating a structured environment include having an area of their bathroom set up with everything they need to get ready, having a dedicated reading and studying area free of any distractions, and putting their books, notepad, pencils, and everything they need in that dedicated space. Additionally, you can set up a place for hanging up their backpack and coat after school and having designated places for toys and shoes to help them develop routines for putting belongings back in the same place so they are less likely to be lost.

In our discussion of scaffolding later in this book, we present the idea that by creating routines, providing reminders, and creating a structured environment will help you support your child where they need help and allow them to stand on their own where they don't need assistance. Greater competence in these areas will build your child's confidence as well.

Prepare for Transitions

When I was around ten years old, I remember watching TV one day before Mom was going to take me to a Fun Night at the elementary school I attended. She was signed up to work a booth or two, and I had asked if I could go with her. Later that night, I was taking a break from my TV show but couldn't find her anywhere. My father then told me she had left without me. I was pretty upset that I missed it, but he said she had asked me three or four times before she left, and I did not respond.

For someone without ADHD, it can be challenging to understand why children with ADHD struggle to switch between tasks. To you and me, transitions might seem like hearing a command and then switching tracks, but to them, the process looks more like this:

1. Initially, they must first recognize that someone is trying to speak to them. It is best to come closer to your child and get their attention—say their name and gently tap their shoulder or touch their hand. Avoid yelling across the room; your presence makes the input stronger.

2. Following the acknowledgment, their brain must process that a person is speaking directly to them. In other words, hearing you talk is only noteworthy if they know

that you are trying to speak to them and it's not just background noise. Ask, "Can we talk for a minute?" to make sure they're listening.

3. Next, actively break their concentration on the current task. Encourage them to put down the iPad or controller and gently guide their hands down from it.

4. Upon breaking concentration, your child must again process what was said, which often involves you repeating yourself. Ask if they understood or are confused and ask questions to test that retention. If they need help understanding, kindly and patiently reiterate your points.

5. Successfully transitioning requires your child's full attention to engage with the new task or communication effectively.

Use Visual Cues/Reminders

We all benefit from little reminders throughout the day. Not just for tasks but to ensure we don't miss our favorite show, remember what we need to pick up at the grocery store on our way home from gymnastics class, or when it is time to take dinner out of the oven. Like us, children need reminders too. There are usually parents providing a gentle nudge to get ready for bed or to clean their room. Alarms and timers can help, but as you can imagine, children with ADHD need reminders as well. Sometimes, using visual cues can help them remember what is expected.

A good strategy is to place visual checklists in the environment in which they are expected to perform a particular task. Having a designated area in their bathroom is a good star, but at first it may take creating a visual chart of each step for them to understand the goal. For instance, a checklist would have pictures of each step to make it is easy for them to remember them. This could just be a small clipart-style picture of someone putting toothpaste on a toothbrush. Then, a picture of the areas of the mouth (fronts, backs, sides, and tongue!). Then, a little picture of a kid flossing, etc.

Using Real Pictures for Visual Cues

A good strategy for teaching organization and memory skills is to take a picture of your child's room and draw *zones* around different areas. Use varying color for each zone, such as blue for the bed, green for the rug, yellow for the dresser, orange for the shelves, etc. Then, when it is time to clean their room, you can refer to the zone you want them to focus on, and they will have this picture to know how the zone should look once it is clean.

The objective is to make your child more independent. By chunking the room into zones and using visual cues, you can avoid overwhelming your child by saying, "Go clean your room." Instead, you can tell them to clean up the blue and green zones and then take a break, reducing your involvement but still providing scaffolding support.

Planning for Sensory Needs

High energy levels are common among children with ADHD, which can be challenging to manage. In fact, their parents can often suffer from exhaustion, highlighting the importance of managing their child's energy levels and parental burnout.

Simultaneously, do not deny your child the opportunity to attempt to meet their own sensory needs. They may need to fidget or move around to feel comfortable, focused, and emotionally stable. You can discourage such behaviors by encouraging physical outlets elsewhere, but outright denying your child the ability to rock back and forth or engage in other stimulation motions can harm them.

First, a rocking chair or an exercise ball might be tremendously helpful to your child. Rhythmic movements can help to reduce excess energy. Although more expensive, therapy swings are available that you can set up at home. Finally, some therapists recommend weighted vests and blankets. Many children respond well to physical pressure, which can help regulate their nervous system.

Targeted Behavior

- **Description of the behavior:**
  - Inappropriately high energy levels.
- **What does this look like?**
  - Restlessness, carelessness, fidgeting, squirming, getting up and moving around instead of staying seated, running or climbing at inappropriate times, talking too much, and interrupting others, distracting others.
- **Why is it undesirable?**
  - Risk or injury to themselves or others.
  - Subsequent damage to furniture and belongings.
  - Parental exhaustion/burnout.
  - Difficulty with peer relationships.

Example Tools and Strategies

- Provide numerous opportunities for physical activity throughout the day. Outdoor play, sports, or simple exercises can channel excess energy positively. Children need creative outlets in which to express themselves, and in doing so, help expel excess energy. For instance, expressing their emotions through music or art can improve their ability to understand emotions without them manifesting as explosive energy.

- Step in and advocate for your child at school—which will likely make their teacher's job easier. Mention that your child has ADHD and needs accommodations like breaks or alternative seating options to remain on task without interrupting others. If your child was formally diagnosed with a learning disability, you might be able to get these accommodations guaranteed through a 504 or Individualized Education Plan (IEP).

- Also, if your child struggles to maintain a consistent energy level yet has disturbingly high energy, try altering the energy levels of different activities throughout the day. For example, follow some silent studying with a physically taxing activity, then encourage winding down after expending the excess energy to help them stabilize their energy levels and will work to avoid hyperactivity at inappropriate times.

Key Takeaways from this Chapter

The main points we want you to leave this chapter knowing are:

1. Routines are one of the most impactful changes you can make in your child's day to help them grasp areas such as planning, organization, time management, emotional control, and working memory.

2. Letting them help build their schedule can increase accountability and enable you to recognize which parts of their routine they struggle with.

3. Ensure you provide a structured environment and prepare for transitions. If they are distracted by what's happening around them, your success in getting them from one task or activity to another will be minimal.

4. Visual cues are an excellent tool to help them perform multiple steps in a task and do those steps in order.

ACTIVITY: Identifying Trouble Spots in Your Daily Routine

As a parent, it can be difficult to establish a daily routine only to find out it isn't working. Worst of all, you might not even know where the routine is going wrong. With this activity, you can identify trouble spots within your child's routine and explore how to improve them:

1. Begin by creating a visual schedule of your child's upcoming day such as a timeline that charts the significant activities from waking up to bedtime.

2. Assign a different color to each type of activity (i.e., morning routine, school time, homework, bedtime). Use colors that resonate with your child.

3. Mark each activity with emojis or symbols representing your child's emotional state during that particular task. For example, a smiling face is for enjoyable activities, and a frowning face is for challenging ones.

4. Add notes or highlights to specific activities. These notes can include observations about your child's behavior, any struggles noticed, or comments on what seems to be working well.

5. Sit down with your child and go through the visual routine map together. Ask open-ended questions like, "How do you feel about getting ready for school?" or "Is there anything about bedtime that you find difficult?"

6. After identifying trouble spots, brainstorm together on possible solutions. Work with your child to develop creative ideas to make challenging activities more enjoyable or manageable.

7. Based on the discussion, create an action plan. Establish changes or strategies to address the trouble spots such as adjusting the routine, introducing incentives, adding visual cues, or organizing spaces more effectively.

Chapter 6 – Strategies for Behavior Mastery

"To be nobody but yourself in a world that's doing its best to make you somebody else is to fight the hardest battle you are ever going to fight. Never stop fighting." —E.E. Cummings

In sixth grade, I walked into my homeroom class one Monday to see that my desk had been moved to the back of the room—right next to the teacher's desk. Also, there was now a strange box enclosing three sides of the desk, the three not facing hers. She had brought in a refrigerator box and cut strategically placed holes so I could see her at the front of the classroom but not the other students, and they couldn't see me. When I came home after school that day and excitedly described my new fort...desk...thing, my mom immediately called the principal for a meeting.

The teacher told my mother she spent all her time correcting my behavior. "It is unfair to the other students," she'd say. Therefore, she told us, she's had to resort to extreme measures so the other kids in the classroom have the opportunity to learn. Back in the early

80s people did not consider something like this as maltreatment, but advocating for children with ADHD was also not a common practice.

My point in telling you that story is that people tend to misjudge ADHD behavior as "bad behavior," but it is crucial to recognize the difference. By understanding ADHD behaviors and implementing practical strategies, parents can create a supportive environment that fosters growth and development for their children.

This chapter will distinguish between a misbehaving child and one behaving in response to ADHD symptoms. We will also examine which parenting techniques are better suited for children with ADHD and how scaffolding, chunking, and taking breaks are essential tools to have in your toolbox.

Recognizing ADHD Behavior vs. "Bad Behavior"

It is important to recognize that misbehavior and behavior as a product of ADHD are two very distinct matters. While bad behavior typically results from a lack of discipline, ADHD behavior is the uncontrollable product of a disorder—a lack of impulse control. Specific behaviors are not your child's fault. Therefore, disciplining this behavior with neurotypical parenting practices is indeed counterproductive.

As mentioned earlier, your parenting is not what caused your child's ADHD; however, since children do aim to please their parents, you are the right person to teach them the skills they lack. But by treating an ADHD behavior as "bad," you effectively demonize your child's core traits in a way that harms their confidence, self-esteem, and autonomy. Instead of addressing unwanted behavior this way, we must understand the critical differences between ADHD behaviors and lack of discipline or intentionally acting out. Some commonly misunderstood ADHD behaviors include:

- **Mood swings**: Children with ADHD often experience mood swings that vary greatly, even by the minute. An ordinarily cheery child can become irritated in minutes due to stimulation needs or unmet accommodations.

- **Depression**: Low mood is not the child acting rude or hateful toward you; instead, it is often a side effect of dealing with untreated ADHD, indicating that they may need additional support.

- **Academic troubles**: These are rarely malicious for a child with ADHD. The educational landscape poses unique challenges for them.

- **Sleep issues**: Sleep deprivation can severely alter a person's moods and behavior. Children with ADHD often have trouble falling and staying asleep—especially for those who take stimulant medication.

- **Oppositional behavior**: Kids with ADHD often try to defy authority, but it is not for the reasons that you think. This behavior usually stems from discomfort, overwhelm, or a lack of understanding on the part of the child. Adaptive parenting strategies can help your child understand how to behave better.

- **Immaturity**: Immaturity is a common trait of children with ADHD, but they are not acting immature on purpose. Remember that ADHD causes developmental delays, so you should treat your eight-year-old the same as you would a neurotypical five-year-old—which genuinely is their maturity level.

- **Distractibility**: Kids with ADHD get easily distracted, but not because they *want* to. They sincerely do not have the same focus control mechanisms that you and I do—provided you do not have ADHD yourself.

If you take anything away from this chapter, we want you to understand that you can't fix ADHD behaviors by punishing a child! However, you can create appropriate expectations and support them in building the skills they require to be successful.

Targeted Behavior

- **Description of the behavior:**
  - Acting out, aggression, violence, and general misbehavior.
- **What does this look like?**
  - Lying, stealing, yelling at or hitting/kicking others, defiance, destroying belongings, bullying, biting, pulling hair, throwing things, etc.
- **Why is it undesirable?**
  - Risk or injury to themselves or others.
  - Parental exhaustion/burnout.
  - Difficulty with relationships.

Example Tools and Strategies

- **Preventative**:
  - Start by fostering a positive environment: Positive reinforcement shifts the focus toward acknowledging and celebrating positive behaviors, steering away from a punitive approach.
  - Model a composed behavior and create a calm, positive environment that contributes to a healthier parent-child dynamic.
  - Elevate your communication game by practicing reflective listening skills, using effective body language, and maintaining eye contact.
  - Connect with your child daily: Use connection time to institute a distraction-free interaction guided by the child's interests.
  - Shed unrealistic expectations: Embrace flexibility and acceptance, particularly in sports, academics, and social interactions.
  - Be consistent in your parenting: Maintain a sense of predictability,

reliability, and stability in everything you do. From daily routines to discipline, ensure your child knows what to expect and when.

- **Practice proactive discipline:**
  - Have established house rules: Post them where your child can see and review the consequence with them before you discipline.
  - Give one clear warning when misbehaving and remind them of that specific rule and its consequences.
  - Make sure the "punishment fits the crime." In other words, use logical consequences—don't take all technology away for a month for not helping set the table.
  - Don't discipline out of anger: Stay calm so you don't escalate the situation. Model using a calm, quiet voice and keep your words to a minimum—they may start to tune out if you decide this is the time to lecture them about following rules. And also, yelling only makes things worse, not better.

Holding Your Child Accountable

Your child has their own set of responsibilities, too. Therefore, if they have a robust study system and receive reminders from you, but they forget their homework and get a bad grade, hold them accountable. Explain the natural consequences involved without offering a punishment to help them attach a cause to effect. Ensure that you also refrain from using ADHD as an excuse (i.e., "She could not help it," "It is not his fault"). If you continue using excuses for your child, they will parrot them back anytime they misbehave.

Discipline that is Still OK for Kids with ADHD

Yes, time-outs, loss of privileges, and chores as a discipline are perfectly acceptable forms of discipline for kids with ADHD. But realize that only some tools and strategies will work. You may need to try various discipline strategies before one *sticks*.

Positive Reinforcement vs. Negative Punishments

Positive reinforcement works if the child knows you are genuine and the incentives are consistent—not random. Most kids with ADHD respond well to praise and rewards. However, some focus on negative events in life, such as comments from parents, teachers, and other kids and this is called *negativity bias*. ADHD is already challenging in so many ways. Why would we want fill their heads with criticism? We must support them by building them up! Protect your child's self-esteem. Be patient and understanding as you focus on helping them develop the required skills to succeed. After all, they genuinely want to please you and show you they are improving.

In addition to negativity bias, many children with ADHD also suffer from *rejection-sensitive dysphoria*, which means they take rejection exceptionally hard. I've heard that children with ADHD receive 20,000 more negative messages by age twelve than other kids. So, letting go of the impulse to correct slight infractions is not such a bad idea. Instead, we should focus on how using positive reinforcement and rewards to work on specific behavior problems can be much more effective.

Selective Ignoring

The relationship between you and your child is essential for getting your child to cooperate. Kids with ADHD tend to be reprimanded many times throughout the day. There comes a point where a child can feel like they can do no right and quits trying. Selective ignoring helps you narrow your focus to only the behaviors you are working to improve.

What does this look like? For the moment, ignore insignificant behaviors that will not hurt your child or someone else. It doesn't mean they are getting away with bad behavior but that you are *temporarily* ignoring it. For example, your child rolling their eyes at you or a little whining or complaining are behaviors we can allow while focusing on what is most important—helping them build the skills to control their impulses, emotions, focus, etc.

Scaffolding

When your child has difficulty initiating a task, it is tempting to tell them each step to perform. Instead, the purpose of scaffolding is to prepare your child for independence, to provide only the support required for you to let them complete the task themselves. Homework and school projects are often areas that children with ADHD find difficulty initiating. It might be tempting to take over their homework so it's finished sooner so you can get on with the rest of your day. However, the best approach will require your child to participate in the planning so they know how to approach these situations in the future.

> Children with ADHD receive 20,000 more negative comments by age twelve than other kids!

One strategy is to ask your child a few questions to provide scaffolding. Asking what homework they may have will only encourage them to list tasks. Instead, ask, "What do you need to do first?" Or "What is the easiest thing you can do to get started?" If that doesn't work, you can get them started by visualizing the finished product and planning backward. You might also ask if they understand the assignment or instructions. Perhaps they are stuck because they truthfully don't know what to do. If you get the dreaded "I don't know" response, ask what they do know. You can decipher where the hang-up is and provide scaffolding using open-ended questions. Scaffolding works for any task your child has difficulty starting or completing.

Scaffolding is beneficial as it helps your child understand the purpose behind why they must do things, it helps develop problem-solving skills and recognizing cause-and-effect relationships. The key is to change commands into open-ended questions. It is tempting to tell your kids to do something because you told them. It is exhausting to explain everything all the time, but you will get better cooperation, and your child will better understand when we use open-ended questions.

Instead of telling your child to grab their coat, try asking if they forgot their coat and if they would enjoy being outside for recess. Or, instead of reminding them to grab their permission slip for a field trip, ask if they will be disappointed if they don't get to go on the field trip. You are not trying to be sarcastic but to get them thinking; therefore, be sincere in your tone of voice and body language. Whenever things don't go how your child wants, it also helps to have them evaluate the situation to create self-awareness and better results in the future. Ask questions like:

- "How do you think that went?"
- "Do you think you did well?"
- "What do you think you could have done differently?"

Remember, the purpose of scaffolding is to meet your child where they are with a challenge and then provide them support to get to the next step. As your child gets older, you must give them more opportunities for independence—and to fail. They need to learn that we learn from the mistakes we make.

Chunking

Trying to start a new habit can be overwhelming, especially if you have ADHD. We are often too ambitious and fizzle out quickly. For example, when January comes around, you set a new year's resolution to exercise more. You get a gym membership and promise to go five times a week for an hour. At first, you do pretty well, but gradually, you go fewer days until March arrives, and you have forgotten your resolution.

It will take a long time to make a new skill a habit. Instead of going big, go small. To start, create tiny goals that feel achievable. Start with pushups for one minute every day for a month. You can be more specific about when (maybe right before bed). Are you going to see massive gains from this? No, but you are creating a habit. Once that is a part of your routine, you can add another goal/skill.

For your child, this might be a desire to improve their grades. Pick what you think will have the most significant impact. For example, if your child frequently forgets to turn in assignments, find a goal that relates to doing homework every night. Instead of making the goal turning in homework, choose the steps your child can succeed at every day. It could be remembering to do homework at least three days a week. The main thing to remember is that the goal needs to be clear and specific and something your child can be successful at.

Another way to use chunking is to break down long-term task/projects. You want to work with your child to break down each task needed to complete the project. Set deadlines for each piece and have a daily plan that focuses on what your child needs to complete that day. Also, it's helpful to have your child take ownership so they can determine what is manageable for them.

You act as a coach, helping them ask the right questions, then check their daily plan and modify it accordingly. But don't fuss at your child if they don't meet the intended target. Try to help them figure out what they must do differently and make a plan for it to happen. Ensure you notice and reward them when making these small steps. It does matter to them!

Your child might be resistant to starting a new habit. It would help you to get buy-in so they take ownership. Having your child explain what they want and how this habit will help them get there is a great idea. Help them realize they will never feel like doing homework, cleaning their room, or working on a school project. They need to break it down into tasks that don't feel overwhelming and do them, get them over with so they can move on to something more engaging.

They also might have self-limiting beliefs, such as being stupid, lazy, or incompetent. You must encourage them to develop a growth mindset instead. Say things like, "This will be hard; you're going to have to push through and keep going, but if you do, think how proud you will be!" Start with what they think they can do and once they do it, encourage them to do a little more each time. "Great job! You wrote a sentence for your paper. Can you write one more?" If they say "No." ask, "Well, can you think about what your next sentence might talk about?" Come up with questions that will push them just a little further. However, if you encounter resistance, praise them for what they have completed and return to it later.

Taking Breaks

Living with executive function deficits can be severely challenging and exhausting for your child. So, it is vital to encourage them to take breaks when needed, especially during tasks they find incredibly taxing, like homework or cleaning. A good example is to have them perform some physical activity or play a game with them. I used to play "I Spy" with my kids, or a game of tag, or toss a ball around in the yard for a few—all beautiful examples of break-time activities that can keep your child engaged and focused during longer tasks requiring their attention. But be mindful that letting your child engage in a preferred activity could trigger hyperfocus.

Key Takeaways from this Chapter

The main points we want you to leave this chapter knowing are:

1. We must recognize the difference between when a child misbehaves and when behavior directly results from a lack of self-restraint, emotional self-regulation, or ability to control their energy or attention due to their disorder.

2. Proactively address behaviors by not waiting until the middle of a struggle with your child to address them.

3. The best discipline strategy to use for a child with ADHD is positive reinforcement. Kids with ADHD get so much negative attention! They don't need someone constantly harping on them for everything they do wrong.

4. Scaffolding is a technique through which you can learn to meet your child where they are in their journey and assist them with achieving independence in their tasks. Doing it for them, having a hands-off approach, or thinking tough love is the best method of parenting are typically not going to work with a child with ADHD.

ACTIVITY: Analyzing Your Child's Behavior: Part II

This activity is about prioritizing what you identified as concerning in Chapter 1, including the "*Analyzing Your Child's Behavior: Part I*" and the example *ABC Chart* we included. Now, it is time to look deeper at that data and develop a plan to improve one of the behaviors.

Follow these steps to guide you:

1. Prioritize behaviors by significance and impact on your child's executive function.

2. Choose the top concern that you believe would make a meaningful difference.

3. Refer to the strategies provided in **Chapters 3** through **6** for managing ADHD behaviors. Choose one strategy, such as creating their daily schedule, adopting declarative language, implementing connection time, etc.

4. Commit to implementing the selected strategy consistently over the next three to four weeks. Recognize that change takes time, and focusing on one behavior and strategy at a time allows for a more practical approach.

Chapter 7 – Strategies for Emotional Regulation and Coping

"It is easier to build strong children than to repair broken men."

—Frederick Douglass

C hildren with ADHD do not experience emotions the same way we do. For a child with ADHD, the emotional landscape can be pretty tricky to manage without the proper skills. As a result, the internal emotional world of your child can manifest outwardly as challenges, behavioral issues, and more. To help your child with emotional regulation, you must first understand your child's unique emotional challenges. Here are examples of the most common challenges:

- **Similar emotions, intensified experience**: Children with ADHD experience the same range of emotions as their peers but with more frequency, intensity, and prolonged duration.

- **Quick and overwhelming response:** They may experience emotions more quickly and become more easily overwhelmed, resulting in big, exaggerated overreactions to ordinary situations.
- **Difficulty with self-soothing:** It takes them longer to calm down, and they may find it challenging to let go of grudges or negative emotions which can develop into frequent temper tantrums or, worse, emotional meltdowns.
- **Impact on relationships:** Controlling intense feelings can be particularly challenging. Quick anger and difficulty managing emotions can impact their relationships, making it crucial to address emotional regulation.

Emotional Dysregulation and Meltdowns

Emotional dysregulation is a hallmark sign of ADHD. Countless studies have shown that children with ADHD struggle the most with impatience, excitability, and frustration. But you should know that emotional challenges are not your child's fault—they do not *want* to be complicated. Remember that they have shortfalls in their executive function. Such emotional challenges begin in the brain—the neural connections of a child with ADHD do not always communicate emotional signals adequately. Intense emotions flood their minds like a dam with a massive hole in it.

Because of these differences in brain structure and chemistry, seemingly insignificant events can turn into catastrophic emotional meltdowns. Children with this issue genuinely cannot help the emotional dysregulation they are suffering from. Combined with a deficit in time-management skills, it makes sense why delayed rewards do not register for kids with ADHD. It is like when my son hears me say "later," he instantly interprets it as "never" and triggers an emotional response.

Different executive functioning skills affect emotional regulation differently. For example, a lack of self-awareness caused by a deficit in metacognition skills will prevent a child from being able to pause, assess what is happening, and reflect on how they should react. Also, unable to prioritize or "calculate the costs" of responding in a specific way will hinder their ability to act appropriately.

Being easily frustrated, having a quick temper, responding with knee-jerk reactions when someone criticizes them, or being extremely sensitive to rejection are all additional examples of a deficit in executive functioning skills. Putting all of this together and behaving with skill in this area is not something that comes naturally to a child with ADHD. They may learn some of these skills over time, but they are developmentally behind their peers, so the expectation that they will behave in a specific way at the same age as others is unrealistic.

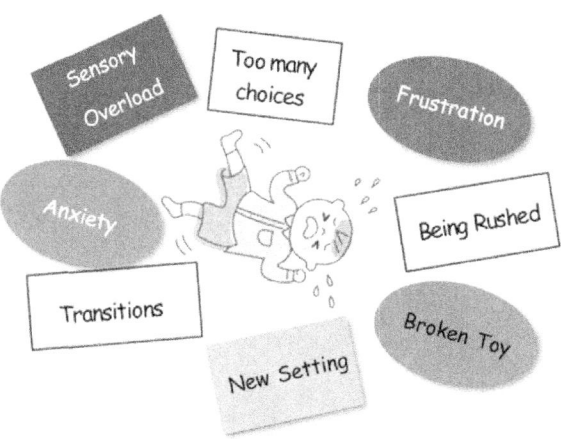

Tantrums vs. Meltdowns

No doubt you have seen a child throw a temper tantrum; most children have them as toddlers. But witnessing an absolute meltdown can be pretty shocking. Imagine parents who deal with meltdowns on a weekly or even daily basis! To understand why this happens, it is essential also to understand the difference.

The key to managing these emotional outbursts is being proactive vs. reactive. If you diligently develop executive function, you will be much more successful in the near and long term. So, spend time with them, focusing on triggers such as transitions or not getting what they want. Work with them on identifying emotions, practicing self-talk and using breathing techniques, and pausing to think about how they will respond when they are triggered. You can model most of this by doing it yourself and talking out loud so they can hear and see you doing what you teach them.

In the following diagram, notice where the two circles intersect and their commonalities. Some event or trigger, called an antecedent, drives both tantrums and meltdowns, and both involve a lack of emotional regulation skills. Now, we can understand why developing these skills and helping your child identify the triggers that cause them to have emotional outbursts are so critical.

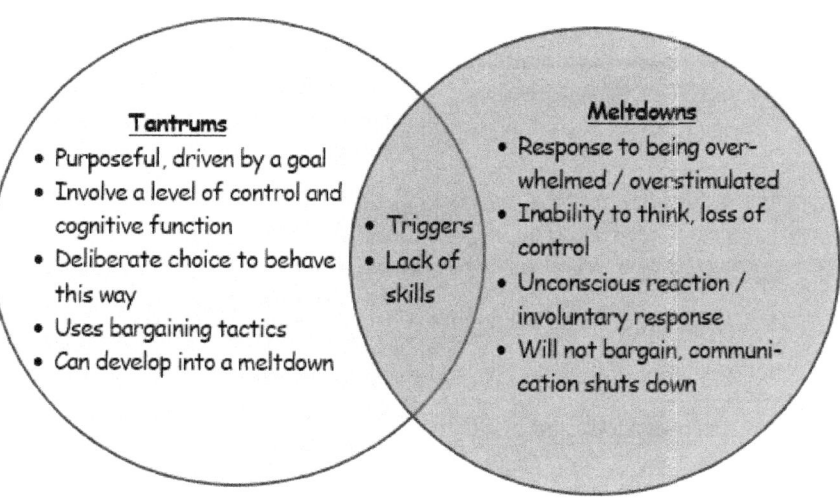

For the most part, such difficulties require a multi-modal approach that emphasizes several strategies for emotional success. Some are tools we mentioned in previous chapters when we talked about emotional control and what it looks like. But what happens when situations get out of control, like when you are in public, and temper tantrums or emotional meltdowns occur? Here are tools we suggest to manage these situations; some preventative and others corrective:

Targeted Behavior

- **Description of the behavior:**
  - Temper tantrums, emotional meltdowns.
- **What does this look like?**
  - A child is screaming, crying, and behaving in erratic manners, potentially even hitting, kicking, throwing, and damaging property or harming people and could happen at home, school, playground, grocery store, visiting friends or neighbors, etc.
- **Why is it undesirable?**
  - Risk or injury, to themselves or others.
  - Parental exhaustion/burnout.
  - Difficulty with all relationships.

Example Tools and Strategies

- **Preventative:**
  - Teach your child mindfulness and relaxation techniques to aid in emotional regulation. Introduce deep breathing, focused awareness, and muscle relaxation techniques.
  - Create visual tools and use timers to help your child build time-management skills, such as understanding the passage of time and estimating how long tasks take to accomplish for transitions between activities, unforeseen changes, not getting their way, and other triggers that might set them off.
  - Use role-play scenarios to simulate real-life situations that trigger intense emotions, which allows your child to practice appropriate responses and coping strategies in a controlled setting.

- Create calming zones which are designated areas in the home or classroom where your child can retreat when feeling overwhelmed, equipped with sensory tools or items that provide comfort.
- Encourage communication: Foster open communication about emotions. Prompt your child to express their feelings and provide a safe space to share their experiences and challenges.

- **Corrective:**
  - Stay calm: Manage your emotions so you don't escalate the situation and model breathing slowly for them. Use a quiet, calm voice and keep your words to a minimum—they are not ready to listen. Yelling or matching their heightened emotions makes it worse.
  - Distract them: In their toddler years, distracting them when something triggers them or drawing their attention to something different can work well with strong emotions. Just don't try to pull this on your teenagers; they may feel insulted and start ignoring you.
  - Ignore it: If you are home or in a place where ignoring the tantrum and allowing it to take its course is possible, do that. Don't give in or provide any acknowledgement that they are behaving this way. Then, praise them when they finish and focus on developing executive function such as labeling the emotion, talking about the trigger, and role-playing to help them decide better behaviors when triggered. But do not consistently ignore temper tantrums without providing the skill-building support they need. Your child needs your attention and ignoring them is denying it. So, be proactive and help them develop their emotional self-regulation sills.
  - Move them to a safe place: If your child is becoming aggressive and

could potentially hurt themselves or others, move them to a safe location. Let them finish their tantrum and follow the above steps to encourage executive function building. Although inconvenient for you, if you have to leave the shopping cart where it is and leave the store, do it! Their safety is more important than the groceries.

Other Strategies for Developing Emotional Regulation

Through the toddler and early school years, modeling behaviors, self-talk, and role-playing are some of the best tools at your disposal. Help your child think of activities they can do when they experience strong emotions. Ask if they need to be alone or if they want a hug. Have them pick something they like to do, such as journal, shoot baskets, kick a ball, draw, read, or listen to music when they recognize something is triggering them, and praise them when you notice them making good decisions.

You can also create a visual reminder for them. Take pictures of them doing these activities and post them in a calm-down area, playroom, or bedroom as a visual prompt of what they can do. Remind them of these activities when you notice they are becoming dysregulated. Once an outburst has passed, help your child reflect on how they handled their emotions. Ask them questions such as, What do they think they did well, and what could they do differently? Did the intensity of their feelings match the situation?

Teach your child to pause and think before responding to something that may have triggered them. Discuss how to consider consequences before reacting. You can help them develop these skills by sharing your thoughts out loud. For example, "I'm angry that my friend backed out on our plans tonight. I will wait before responding to her text so I don't say something that might hurt our friendship."

Addressing Emotional Dysregulation as a Family

Emotional outbursts can take a toll on parents. However, it can also have significant effects on other family members. Below are more tools to help your family when your children struggle to handle their emotions:

Tap In / Tap Out

Sometimes, when a child is experiencing emotional dysregulation, they may want your presence to help them calm down. Other times, they prefer to be alone, away from everyone else, or just away from the person bothering them. Your child can tell you they want to "tap in" or "tap out," or you can ask what they want. A tap in might look like snuggling on the couch for a few minutes, rubbing your child's back, or any other quiet activity your child enjoys with you. A tap out would involve each of you going somewhere to be alone for a few minutes to do a calming activity.

Your child could go listen to music, read a book, journal, shoot baskets, or draw; not as a punishment, but as their choice for how they want to self-regulate. Avoid checking on them every few minutes. Once everyone is relaxed, you can discuss what happened, any consequences, and how your child can handle the situation better.

The Family Sync

The family sync is an excellent toll to create a plan ahead of time for future emotional events. Getting your children involved in the solution will increase the likelihood of their cooperation. Gather everyone together when everyone is calm and happy (not just right after a meltdown). Keep the meeting short, about 15 minutes. Use this time together to examine what situations usually cause emotional dysregulation. What responses decrease the intensity of the emotions, and what escalates them? What helps your child calm down? Do they prefer a tap-in or a tap-out? How long does it usually take before they calm down?

Create a chart as a visual reminder of what everyone will do and post it somewhere they can see. Meet back again in the future to make modifications as necessary.

A Free Pass / Free Take-back

Have you ever said something and immediately wished you could take it back? A free pass is an opportunity to take something back you said, ask forgiveness if necessary, and rephrase what you said to something more helpful. Your child gets one free pass a day, meaning there will not be a consequence for the behavior because they recognized they made a mistake and tried expressing their feelings more appropriately. You can model this for your child by apologizing when you lose your cool and saying something hurtful by rephrasing to something more appropriate. Then, ask them if you can use your free pass for the day. They will learn this method for apologizing when they've lashed out.

Practice Runs

If you have identified situations that usually cause emotional dysregulation for your child, you can do practice runs where they can earn rewards for keeping calm. Pick a time when you are not in a hurry and you don't have plans. For example, if your child has difficulty stopping a preferred activity, have them engage in the activity and practice stopping after a few minutes. If they remain calm and stop the activity, give them a small reward. If needed, break the task into smaller parts, focus on one until mastered, and then add the other steps. For example, if your child struggles with your morning routine, take one step in the routine and practice it. Start with whichever step in the routine is causing the issue.

Having an Emotional Plan of Action

Help your child identify situations that often cause emotional dysregulation (feeling like people aren't listening to them, when they have to leave a fun activity or place, when someone laughs at them, etc.). After listing those triggers, identify people they can go to for help, places to calm down, and activities they can do to calm down. Be specific to that situation. For example, they can't go to one of their parents for help if it occurs at school. When home, they can go to their bedroom or outside to get fresh air. If they are at school, they might have to talk to their teacher about a place in the classroom, the rules for using that space, other options, and when they can use them. Choose activities that work for that location and situation.

Have multiple strategies the child can try. As they try them, remove ones that aren't helpful and try new ones. This plan is constantly evolving. As your child identifies new triggers, include those in the plan. If your child deals with worry or anxiety, emotional plans of action can be extremely beneficial. Talk with your child about what is coming up that is causing them worry. Plan ahead of time how they can cope. If you notice they struggle to manage their emotions when the situation arrives, remind them about their plan and the coping strategies they will try.

Key Takeaways from this Chapter

The main points we want you to leave this chapter knowing are:

1. Kids with ADHD have more difficulty coping and controlling their emotions than other kids. Being proactive vs. reactive will go a long way when helping them identify triggers and calm themselves down.
2. Get your family involved in helping you address emotional dysregulation. Teach everyone the skills you teach your child so they can help, too.

Fun Breathing Styles

 ## Balloon Breathing

1. Sit or lie down and put one hand on your tummy.
2. Inhale slowly through your nose—feel your tummy rise like a balloon!
3. Hold your breath for a moment
4. Then exhale slowly through your mouth—imagine a balloon deflating!
5. Repeat this five times.

 ## Bumble Bee Breathing

1. Take a deep breath in through the nose.
2. Make a humming or buzzing sound like a bee!
3. Keep buzzing while you breathe out.
4. Repeat this five times.

 ## Starfish Breathing

1. Spread their fingers wide, making a starfish shape!
2. Take a deep breath and spread your fingers out.
3. Breathe out and bring your fingers back together.
4. Repeat this five times.

 ## Bubble Breathing

1. Grab a bubble wand and some bubble solution.
2. Breathe in deeply through your nose.
3. Breathe out slowly while blowing bubbles.
4. Repeat this as many times as you want! ☺

Chapter 8 – Strategies for Building Social Skills and Friendships

"I would rather walk with a friend in the dark than walk alone in the light." —Helen Keller

Most people agree that friendships and social skills are crucial for fulfillment and are the crux of positive interactions. But for a child with ADHD, making friends and socializing with others can be one of the most complex parts of growing up. Fortunately, social skills can be improved, thus, improving positive friendships.

Social awkwardness and the criticism from others can make children with ADHD feel "weird," which underscores the need for a more empathetic society. The inherent symptoms of ADHD—inattention, hyperactivity, and impulsivity—are enough to make social interactions challenging for your child. This chapter serves as a guide to help you improve your child's ability to interact with other kids.

Besides the tendency to overlook social cues, lack of attention control makes it challenging to listen to others and become easily distracted during conversations.

Hyperactivity can cause frequent interruptions, talking too much, and fixating on a topic. These make it hard for your child to keep up in conversations or for others to keep up with them! Finally, invading others' personal space and starting conversations at inappropriate times are all adverse effects of impulsivity.

Building Social Skills for Positive Friendships

Most counselors agree that one of the primary tools you can use to help your child build everyday social skills is practicing them through role play and interaction with your child. Consistent social skills development can help them learn how to relate to others and empower them to apply those social skills to other situations on their own. Let's look at some strategies you can use:

Strategies to Help Our Child Develop Social Skills

Targeted Behavior

- **Description of the behavior:**
  - Lack of social skills, difficulty making/ keeping friends
- **What does this look like?**
  - Anxiety meeting new peers, not knowing what to do or say when meeting new people, interrupting group activities, not taking turns or not sharing, not being flexible, arguing about opinions/preferences, being bossy or dominating conversations, saying/ doing things at inappropriate times, not able to *read the room* or recognize others' emotions.
- **Why is it undesirable?**
  - Not necessarily an undesirable behavior; as much as we want to see our children develop relationships with others, their deficits in social skills make this more challenging.

Example Tools and Strategies

- **Sharing and turn-taking**: Spend as much time as you can role-playing with your child during board games, sports, video games, etc., where you and your child take turns. You can teach patience and show your child it is OK to wait, which helps teach delayed gratification.

- **Initiating conversation**: Teach them how to meet new people—mainly how to make eye contact, introduce themselves, and respond to others' introductions. Help them understand this is a time to take turns, waiting until it is their turn to speak. Engaging in role-play conversations (i.e., playing chef or teacher) where you take turns talking about who they are, what they like to do, who else they may be playing with that day, what their family is like, etc.

- **Model active listening**: When role-playing social interactions and taking turns with your child, you can model reflective listening for them. Give them your full attention and try to summarize what they tell you. Ask questions that show them you are listening and engaged in what they say. Even if hearing about the new world they built in Minecraft bores you to tears, this is a crucial time for you to develop your relationship.

- **Teach them individuality:** Everyone has different likes, dislikes, tastes, and opinions. Teach them how to talk about those differences and accept them as that person's individual preferences. Teach them that it is OK to have different tastes, that everyone has different opinions, and that all of those unique preferences are what make people special. Use this while watching their favorite show or reading a story so they can connect that skill with a preference of theirs.

- **Collaboration/teamwork:** When starting an activity, such as a collaborative art project or just playing a game that requires teamwork, teach your child the difference between collaboration and competition. These lessons can empower your child to work effectively with others. Also, teach them how to ask to join a game or other group activities that have already started.
- **Social cues:** This is a significant challenge for kids with ADHD. We recommend using cue cards with facial expressions and talking with them about body language. Use those cards to explore social cues and what to expect during social interactions. Focus on personal space and appropriate distances to interact with others.
- **Conflict resolution:** Provide immediate feedback when your child behaves inappropriately during your role-playing and interactions. You can also practice conflict resolution skills and teach your child effective ways to improve their problem-solving skills.
- **Work on improving other areas of executive function**: Improving your child's impulse control, emotional control, cognitive flexibility, and metacognition can improve their social skills and relationships with others. Focus on those areas as you help them develop social skills using the above methods.

As you rehearse these skills with your child, remember that consistency and repetition are invaluable. They need regular exposure to social skills to practice them.

How to be Successful When Working on Social Skills

What if you do not know a skill your child should work on? How can you help them improve their social skills? The method below is a way to focus on those skills:

- **Use targeting**: Break social skills down into specific components and focus on enhancing one skill at a time. Don't try to teach eye contact, introducing themselves, taking turns speaking, active listening, and body language all at once—practice them individually over time until they have learned them.

- **Give them a mission**: Assigning your child social *missions* can be fun for them to learn to observe others in social situations. Have them act like a spy, secretly listening to others without them knowing. Give them specific perspective-taking goals and practice this at school or on the playground. Have them report back to you what they learned. Teach them to read the room and notice details about the environment and people in it.

- **Help them find friends**: Encourage connections with peers who share similar interests. Sign them up for a club that interests them, take them to community events, find Mom groups and see who they connect with. Ask parents if they can get together again if your kids play well together.
  - Before play dates, discuss and plan activities with your child. Ask your child what they might want to do, and then tell them to ask what their friend likes so they can decide together.
  - Choose activities and environments where your child feels comfortable and can talk as they play. Going to a bounce house or other super noisy location to play together removes their ability to interact socially.
  - You can also use subtle cues to indicate to your child when to pause, listen, or respond appropriately.

Remember, the key is consistent practice, patience, and celebrating progress. Social skills are lifelong skills that can be cultivated and refined with ongoing support and guidance. Even if your child still struggles, it is important to discover what works best for them. This means not giving up if you *and* your child are frustrated.

Teaching Empathy and Social Awareness

A balance of empathy and social awareness means that your child understands social needs while being kind to themselves and those around them. An empathetic and socially aware child understands the emotions of others. They also know that Mom does not want them to do chores just to torture them; mom wants them done because it is *important* to her.

One way to help is to vary how you play with your child. Instead of always playing what or how they want to play, take turns deciding what to play. Don't be surprised if this upsets your child—keep trying. You will be more understanding of your child than peers who will get frustrated by their lack of cognitive flexibility.

A great strategy is to read a story and ask them questions about the characters. Examine the emotions of these characters with your child, their social interactions, what they did right or wrong when interacting, how they must feel during a given situation, etc. Encourage them to read the room by seeing how others act and their responses during interactions. Then, encourage your child to practice these approaches in other settings to build confidence and behave appropriately.

Children learn much from fantasy playtime because it makes abstract concepts seem more real. You can help your child learn empathetic responses by creating compassionate role-play scenarios. For instance, you can act out someone's feelings getting hurt. Share real-life examples and talk about the positive impacts of empathy. Discuss how understanding others' feelings contributes to building strong friendships.

As always, encourage your child to share their personal experiences and feelings. Talk about situations where empathy came into play and explore the impact of understanding others' perspectives. Feel free to share your personal experiences with empathy, showing first-hand accounts of empathy to help your child realize that they enjoy empathy when directed at them. So, they should direct it to others.

Your child might also benefit from having their social interactions debriefed. Ask them how different people might have felt in various situations. Doing so gives them direct examples of how their actions create empathy and encourage positive emotions in others.

Social Challenges in Specific Settings

Specific social settings can also prove challenging for children with ADHD. Classroom environments or collaborative group activities such as team sports can be challenging for children who are especially disruptive. You can help by offering structured activities broken into smaller segments and providing positive reinforcement for appropriate behavior.

Additionally, when a child isn't considerate of others' perspectives, it can make them seem insensitive to their values. Frankly, all children can appear rude when they aren't interested in something or when they get distracted. If they have difficulty taking turns, it can make them appear rude or just downright mean. On the other hand, some children get withdrawn and struggle to initiate conversations when asking for help, presenting in front of others, or speaking up in a group. You can help your child improve in these situations by implementing some of the tools mentioned above. By practicing these skills with you, they can build confidence they can apply with peers.

Handling Bullying and Boosting Self-Confidence

Now, let's talk about something many children with ADHD will undoubtedly face during their lifetime, perhaps frequently. As unfortunate as it is, bullying is a common issue faced by kids with ADHD. Your child might not even understand what bullying is or how to stand up for themselves, and as a parent, you might be unsure of what you can do to support your child. If left unaddressed, bullying can lead to physical injuries and emotional distress, or worse. Kids who suffer bullying are also at significant risk for mental health problems.

You must recognize the signs of bullying—and your child does, too. Teach them that bullying has verbal, social, and physical forms. It can go from name-calling or threatening to spreading rumors, shaming someone, or embarrassing them in public, to hitting, pushing, tripping, and even taking or breaking their belongings. Discuss what bullying looks like and focus on how it makes someone feel. Ensure they always feel comfortable discussing experiences with friends and classmates with you. Most importantly, ensure they know you take bullying seriously and can confide in you if they feel bullied.

As a parent, be watchful for signs of bullying. Even if your child does not know it, they will likely behave differently if bullied or treated poorly at school. For instance, they might not want to go to school or even become afraid, making excuses for not going. Their grades might drop uncharacteristically; they may lose interest in areas related to where they are being bullied (school, playground, sports, neighborhood friends). They

> The CDC reports that about 30% of middle schoolers and 20% of high schoolers experience bullying every year.

may even seem sad, moody, or emotionally upset for no apparent reason. If bullying gets worse, you may even see a loss of appetite, have trouble sleeping, or complain of stomachaches or headaches. You must address these signs as soon as you see them.

Unfortunately, you cannot control the behavior of others. You cannot make them stop bullying, so the next best thing is helping your child be resilient. At home, take the time to highlight your child's strengths, boosting their self-esteem and confidence. Be sure to compliment even their more uncharacteristic strengths. This might not seem like a lot, but it can stick with a child in a school hallway. Try to dissuade negative self-talk and encourage a healthy self-image.

Moreover, your child has to learn to be assertive. This can be helpful if you focus on teaching assertiveness, emotional expression skills, and how to set boundaries with other children. Your child should know when to feel comfortable saying, "I do not like how you are treating me; please stop." They also need to know there's a difference between "tattling" and reporting bullying and that they should 100% do the latter.

Even if you do everything right, your child may face unavoidable, hurtful situations. They may not be telling you everything—children can be rather cunning about their bullying habits. Therefore, your child should have an arsenal of coping skills ready for such situations:

- **Problem-solving**: Help your child understand problem-solving skills to navigate challenging situations. Help them identify responses to bullying for coping and avoiding bullying behavior.
- **Role-playing**: Practice scenarios with them to learn responses to bullying. Teach them how to confidently assert themselves while seeking help from trusted adults. Work on some *tease-proof* tactics to help them ignore teasing from peers and teach them how to respond effectively to teasing.
- **Encourage support seeking**: Reinforce the importance of seeking out teachers, school counselors, and other trusted adults when facing bullying. Let your child know they are not alone in dealing with the situation.

There is no shame in collaborating with the school. You can keep an open line of communication with your child's teacher, allowing you to ask about your child's social experiences so that you know what's going on and can express any concerns you have. Please make sure that you hold the school accountable for bullying control and discuss strategies to create a safe and supportive environment for your child.

Parents also have the power to advocate for anti-bullying initiatives within the school. Support and participate in programs that promote a culture of kindness, empathy, and inclusion. The school can be a more positive place for children.

If you allow your child access to social media or technology like multiplayer video games, you must be on your toes regarding cyberbullying. Inform your child about responsible online behavior, and encourage them to report any instances of cyberbullying. This involves setting clear guidelines for your child's online activities, monitoring their online interactions, and guiding them in maintaining healthy boundaries in the digital space. Be aware of cyberbullying trends, too. If cyberbullying occurs within the school community, the school authorities should be addressing the issue.

Key Takeaways from this Chapter

The main points we want you to leave this chapter knowing are:

1. Most people agree that building friendships is one life's most important ways to feel fulfilled. But for children with executive function deficits, this is easier said than done. The best way to address social dysfunction is by using proactive methods to prepare them.

2. Many skills children with ADHD need do not come naturally; they must be learned. This will mostly come from you as a parent, modeling socially acceptable behavior, talking out loud to describe what you are doing, teaching social cues and body language, and helping with positive conflict resolution.

3. There are times when you should do what your child wants when you play with them, and other times where you must model appropriate flexibility so they don't throw a fit every time life doesn't go their way.

4. Around 30% of middle schoolers are victims of bullying. Teach your child to recognize the right way to treat people vs. when someone is bullying. Build their resilience so they know how to handle being bullied.

ACTIVITY: Friendship Wheel

Have your child reflect on their current friends and learn to value positive friendships. Draw a circle and divide it into four or six sections. Encourage them to write the name of a friend and the quality that they like best in each section.

If you notice your child picked someone you do not think behaves like a friend, examine with them what behaviors they want their friends to have—and which they don't. We recommend not telling them that person isn't a friend. The idea is to get them thinking about what qualities good friends should have.

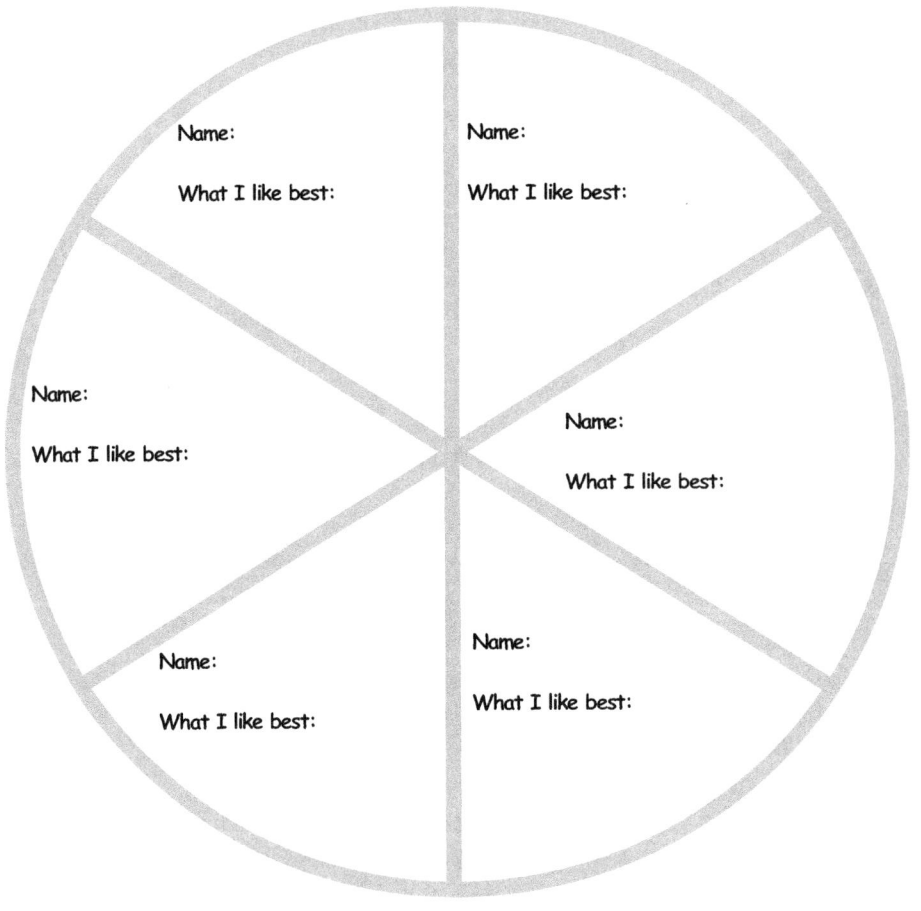

Chapter 9 – Strategies for Academic Success

"Everybody is a genius. But if you judge a fish by its ability to climb a tree, it will live its whole life believing that it is stupid."

—Albert Einstein

Academic success is important in a society. It is essential for success in the workplace and personal situations. At the same time, it is a significant struggle for kids with ADHD, so you must meet your child halfway, which means we should be encouraging them to do their best and supporting them where they are struggling. It is crucial to communicate frequently with your child's teacher so you can share what strategies and techniques are working and where to adjust. This chapter will discuss extra age-appropriate strategies you can use to empower your child to succeed in academics.

How Parents Can Help Their Child at Home

When your child begins attending school, you will oversee their organization and planning. Essentially, you will be their executive function system. Therefore, aim to set routines in place that will help your child be successful. Things to consider include:

- Maintaining consistency in a morning routine
- Establishing a designated area of the home for a backpack
- What to do when getting home from school
- Adding events to the calendar
- Communicating with the teacher.

Use visual reminders so your child can see what they must do. As they get older, have them get involved in the organization and planning so that they are completely independent by the time they graduate from high school. However, your child will need your involvement for a while, so you have plenty of time to prepare them.

Homework

For starters, your child needs your help creating a home environment conducive to learning. You can create a home environment that enables your child to learn by designating a well-lit, clean, distraction-free study space. A desk for studying is perfect, but ensure to limit background noise, turn off unnecessary electronics, and provide tools like noise-canceling headphones if needed. Also ensure supplies are kept in this area so your child doesn't get distracted looking for a pencil.

You can also set up a system for taking breaks. Help your child develop a list of short activities (about ten minutes) they can do in between homework assignments. Don't pick activities that are too long or too difficult to pull them away from. For example, my son would choose video games, but I know it will be too hard to pull him away and get him to focus on schoolwork again. However, it should be a preferred activity to be truly motivating. I would like him to exercise, but that was another activity he disliked, so it wasn't a good choice.

Next, determine when they get to take the break. For example, it could be after 30 minutes of work or once they complete two tasks. Keep modifying until you find what works best for you and your child.

Your child will probably need your help breaking down some assignments into smaller parts, especially for long-term projects. Use the chunking strategies mentioned previously to help with task initiation and prevent overwhelm.

Body Doubling

Having someone sit with your child while they work is called *body doubling*. The person does acts not as a taskmaster but as a nearby, calming presence. They can read a book, scroll on their phone, or do any other quiet activity. However, have them avoid watching television or washing dishes, as these activities would be distracting. For older children, this can be a peer so long as they are there to work on schoolwork.

Daily/Weekly Schedule

As kids approach middle school, you can help them create daily and weekly plans. Start with the weekly plan and include everything that is coming up that week, including sports practices, music lessons, school activities, family events, school projects, chores, and plans with friends. Then, help them make a plan for the next day. Discuss what they think is the top priority that day?

You can also sequence them chronologically to specify when your child will do them. Have them estimate how long activities will take and reflect on whether their estimate was accurate. Once you have made the plan, have them tell you what the plan is for the next day. Designate a visible location to keep it posted. In the morning, have your child look at the plan and tell you what two activities they will do when they get home from school. At the end of the day, talk about what went well that day, what did not, and how to improve it next time. This reflection is an important step, so try to complete it. Then, help them make their plan for the next day.

In the beginning, this will take considerable time and effort. Still, as your child consistently practices, you can step back and be amazed at how independently they manage their schedule. Remember, only provide the support your child needs; you should aim is to move them to the next step towards independence.

Your child probably doesn't enjoy doing homework or other non-preferred tasks, so talk to them about how they will stick to the plan even when they don't want to. Maybe they can develop a phrase to get them through it, like "Just get it done so I can have fun." Or maybe, "Once I complete two tasks, I can take a break to do something fun." Our son always says, "This isn't that much; I can do this!" Develop some tools to help motivate your child to stick to the plan. Get them involved in coming up with ideas of what will work for them. Here are a few tools you can use to help your child stay on top of their school requirements:

- When they get home from school, have them go through their backpacks with you. Take out anything that isn't needed, such as already graded assignments. Look for teacher notes and at their homework assignments for that night so you can help them remember to do them.
- Check the student's online school portal regularly to ensure there aren't any notices of missing assignments. Investigate any low grades or notes from teachers. Then, take a look at upcoming assignments.
- Instead of waiting to talk to a teacher about something, you can email them for clarification about an assignment or how to improve a grade.

- Make a daily plan/schedule to refer to when they can't remember. What is the top priority for today? What other tasks do you need to complete?

Addressing Problem Areas

To understand where to focus your efforts, we should examine some of the executive functioning skills involved. By now, you should be able to spot these and know why they can create problems for your child—deficits in organization, planning, task initiation, time management, working memory, etc. As a parent, you can help troubleshoot where the disconnect occurs.

Is your child forgetting they have homework to do? Are they struggling with studying for tests? Are they failing to turn in assignments? Help them devise a plan to address the problem and set a goal. You might walk them through creating a checklist to carry with them that they can refer to often so they remember the steps.

Once you have identified what your child will work on, set the goal and help them determine what they think they can realistically succeed at. For example, if your child struggles to get started on homework, that goal might be to start homework at a specific time for three days of the week. Do not make turning their homework in the goal unless it is the only area of concern. Be more specific—the ultimate goal is turning it in, but focus on which step is causing the immediate problem.

As your child masters a goal repeatedly, make it more challenging or move on to the next step, causing issues with handing in homework. As mentioned, choose an incentive that motivates your child and include them in deciding what it will be. Don't be surprised if there are setbacks and you need to return to a previous target goal. But always remember to praise your child for their success.

Targeted Behavior

- **Description of the behavior:**
  - o Lack of responsibility/ accountability.
- **What does this look like?**
  - o Forgetfulness, carelessness, losing personal belongings, not taking care of others' belongings, not remembering tasks or inability to stay organized.
- **Why is it undesirable?**
  - o Difficulty with academics (classroom assignments/ tests), bad grades.
  - o Lack of responsibility for their belongings or those of others.
  - o Damaged relationships due to carelessness and losing belongings.

Example Tools and Strategies

- **Make sure the basics are cared for**: proper sleep, regular exercise, a healthy diet, and routines and structure in the home are crucial if we want our child to succeed academically.

- **Designate a study area**: Work with your child to create a dedicated study area at home, free of distractions. A quiet and organized space can enhance focus. Encouraging your child to work in the same place every time can ensure that new settings are not distracting.

- **Provide proper supplies**: Make sure their study area is equipped with necessary supplies which should encourage students to take charge of their learning experience rather than having to ask you for this, that, and the other during their study times.

- **Collaborate with teachers**: Asking your child's teacher(s) for support can be invaluable when organizing home life. You can ask for simple accommodations, like extra reminders to write assignments down, that make study sessions more fruitful.

- **Review their homework**: Before the next school day, review homework assignments and make sure that materials are pre-packed for the next school day to ensure your child will not be rummaging to find things at school or even forgetting them on the way out the door.
- **Color code supplies**: Children love colorful supplies, so why not make them functional? Color coding supplies, such as blue for English and red for match, can help your child understand transitions between subjects.
- **Motivating reward system**: Ensure your child has some incentive for their efforts, encouraging them to work harder and harder.

How Parents Can Help Their Child at School

Your child's academic success will require collaboration between you and the school. Let the teacher know if something is going on at home that your child is struggling with. Consider sharing strategies you use at home that might help at school. If homework is taking hours every night, let the teacher know. They may be asking for too much and can possibly shorten assignments. The aim is that your child is progressing, and if the teacher sees their effort, they will most likely be accommodating.

Since communication is so important, your child's teacher might use a daily report card or other means to contact you about how your child is doing during the school day. The daily report card is an effective school-based intervention that provides an easy means for parents and teachers to communicate about your child's progress on behavioral goals at school. Some behaviors it might address are homework completion, arguing with the teacher, interrupting, following directions, having class materials, and more. The behaviors are specific and observable by the teacher. They usually choose between 3-5 behaviors only and make sure the goals are achievable.

Once goals have been established, you and your child can meet with the teacher to ensure expectations are clear and understood. The teacher may use classroom incentives for younger children, but you will provide the necessary support at home for older children.

Other tools the school might use to assist your child's success include:

- Short breaks
- Praise/positive reinforcement
- Additional time to complete assignments or tests
- Fewer problems with homework
- Different seating choices
- Placing a child in the front row or at a table with fewer children

Self-Awareness Activities for Students

You can help your child learn to maintain consistent awareness of themselves and their needs. An example is creating a success file which can be a folder, notebook, or other compilation of your child's successes. Encourage them to create this independently and update it regularly with worksheets, awards, and notes from teachers. Include a checklist of particular struggles and possible solutions. They should outline their own personal learning challenges and support they require from teachers. Thus, they will have a greater awareness of their strengths and weakness and will learn how accommodations can improve their success.

Working With Schools and Utilizing 504 Plans and IEPs

IEPs and 504 plans are two types of accommodations that children with special needs—including those with ADHD—can take advantage of. Legally, a school must follow these plans, as they include demonstrated needs and the accommodations to ensure that your child has a fair educational experience. It is time for you to learn about these accommodations, as you are the parent and, therefore, the primary influencer in getting your child such a plan.

But what is an IEP? They are individualized education programs that are personalized for each child. ADHD is a disability in many ways, and IEPs are created with the explicit intention of making education possible for disabled children by meeting their unique and specific educational needs. It outlines necessary services, accommodations, and goals to support the child's academic success.

Within an IEP, your child will have academic and functional goals, special education services, related services, and accommodations tailored to their unique needs, which every teacher will be informed of. Note that a child with severe ADHD may qualify for an IEP, but it typically means that they also have some form of learning ability as well.

To get an IEP, your child will undergo a comprehensive assessment. This assessment will examine your child's needs, strengths, and weaknesses to determine how the IEP can best achieve their academic success. Parents, educators, and relevant professionals collaborate to develop the IEP, considering the child's current level of performance and setting measurable goals, which means you will play an active role in creating the plan, so understanding your child is crucial.

Getting an IFP formed and implemented for your child comes in two parts: requesting and implementing. You must be present and vocal about your child's needs during both phases. Here is a general overview of the process to request an IEP:

- **Document your child's needs**: Compile documentation highlighting your child's academic and behavioral challenges. Include assessments, teacher observations, and any relevant medical or psychological reports.

- **Collaborate with the teacher**: Meet with their teacher to discuss your shared concerns about their behavior. Examine what strategies have worked and what new strategies could help them in the classroom.

- **Submit a formal request**: A request to evaluate your child for special education services. In this letter, detail your concerns, share supporting documents, and express your desire for collaboration.

- **Evaluation process**: The school will conduct an evaluation, considering input from teachers, parents, and relevant professionals. This process may involve assessments, observations, and discussions for formal documentation to ensure your child's IEP is adequately recorded.

- **IEP meeting**: Once the evaluation is complete, you will be invited to a meeting where the evaluation results will be discussed. Your child's strengths, challenges, problems in the classrooms, and accommodations will all be addressed. You will find out whether the request was approved, and if it was not, you will find out why—and have a chance to contest it.

- **Plan development**: If they determine your child is eligible, you will work collaboratively with the school to create the plan. It will outline accommodations and support services tailored to your child's needs.

Sometimes requests are denied, and you may have to follow an alternate approach. If your child's difficulties do not extend outside of the school, they may recommend a 504 Plan instead. This plan will not have goals or a special education liaison. However, they both provide accommodations that can extend into college years. Remember to be diligent and continue to advocate for your child's needs during the IEP process. Communicate the necessity of an IEP based on your child's specific challenges. Include any documentation that you have, such as medical evaluations.

Parental Advocacy at School

Some tips that can help you advocate for your child and encourage a positive relationship with school include:

- **Know the rules**: Understand the educational laws and policies for children with ADHD. Familiarize yourself with the IEP and 504 Plan processes to encourage fair treatment and accommodation.

- **Get to know those in charge**: Establish a positive relationship with teachers, administrators, and special education staff. Attend parent-teacher conferences and actively engage with the school community.

- **Keep up with your records**: Maintain organized records of your child's academic progress, assessments, and communication with school personnel. This documentation can be valuable during advocacy efforts.

- **Stay informed**: Keep up on the latest information regarding ADHD, its impact on learning, and evidence-based interventions. Share relevant information with educators to enhance their understanding.

- **Communicate**: Foster open and constructive communication with teachers and school staff, clearly expressing your child's needs, strengths, and any concerns you may have.

- **Be solution-focused**: Approach challenges with a solution-oriented mindset. Work collaboratively with educators to find effective strategies that support your child's learning.

- **Let your child be involved**: Encourage your child to be part of the decision-making process. Their insights and preferences are valuable in creating an inclusive and supportive learning environment.

Self-Advocacy in School

At its core, self-advocacy involves expressing one's needs clearly. Your child might understand what they require to succeed in various circumstances, but if they cannot express these needs, they will be unable to advocate for themselves. For children with ADHD, developing self-advocacy skills is especially vital in navigating the complexities of the educational system and social environments.

There are three key elements that you should know to help your child master this ability:

- **Understanding their needs**: Your child needs to understand their needs to communicate them. Encourage your child to reflect on their strengths, challenges, and the specific aspects of learning or social situations that may pose difficulties. Writing this down can be helpful for them.

- **Know what kind of support might help**: Help them brainstorm what might help them the most. For instance, an easily distracted child might benefit from preferential seating where their desk is closer to the front. Specific learning tools, extra time for assignments, and more can also be helpful accommodations.

- **Communicate those needs**: Teach them to communicate their needs clearly and effectively to others.

Key Takeaways from this Chapter

The main points we want you to leave this chapter knowing are:

1. Supporting your child is vital to their success. But know that learning disabilities can accompany ADHD symptoms. So, make sure you identify whether they have challenges with reading, spelling, math, and other areas of academics so you can have them evaluated and get them the proper therapy.

2. Use strategies mentioned in other areas of this book, such as creating a calm environment, eliminating distractions, and building routines and schedules for them to follow to help them succeed with homework and tests.

3. If your child's teacher uses a daily report card or other behavioral goal system to communicate with you about how your child is performing, make sure to check it daily. Praise your child for their accomplishments and talk with them about ideas to help them be more successful at areas they find challenging.

4. If your child's ADHD symptoms are severe and are preventing them from success in the classroom, look into 504 plans and IEPs to see if your child is a good candidate to receive special accommodations.

5. Besides being an advocate for your child, teach them self-advocacy skills so they can reach out when they need help.

Conclusion

Raising a child with ADHD is no easy feat, but if you finished this book, we know you are committed to doing what's best for your child. Your child can successfully feel supported in all areas of life, whether finding the right treatment options, seeking consistency and routine, or just knowing they have a supportive parent in their corner when needed.

We urge you to follow our recommendations for examining your child's behavior to identify which executive functioning skills they struggle with. Develop consistent routines and a structured household. Find out what treatment options are available in your area and speak with a doctor to see which options work best for your child. Choose some tools and strategies to implement to help them improve their executive function, but remember to start small to avoid getting overwhelmed. Be proactive in areas they need help in, such as identifying triggers that set them off. Model self-talk and declarative language when possible so they can learn from you.

As you close the pages of this book, remember that you are not alone in your journey. The community around you, whether family, friends, or support groups, is there to lift you up. Your child's unique strengths and abilities are a gift to be celebrated and embraced. Remember to advocate for your child, nurture their strengths, and be amazed as they thrive despite their ADHD.

Dear Reader,

If you found this book to be insightful, we kindly invite you to consider leaving a review. Knowing that we have been able to help parents in any way would mean the world to us!

https://linktr.ee/adhdparenting

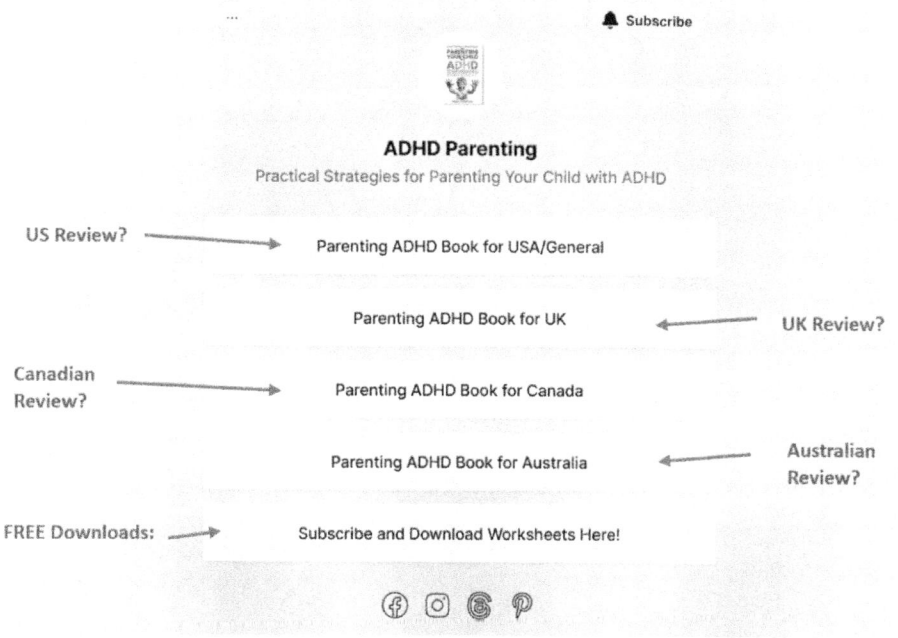

Once again, thank you so much for reading this book! We hope to continue to help others in their journey through life as we continue ours.

With Warm Regards,

Thomas and Carrie Allen

References

12 neurodiversity strengths that come from thinking differently. (n.d.). Texthelp. https://www.texthelp.com/resources/blog/12-neurodiversity-strengths-that-come-from-thinking-differently/

Abigail. (2022, May 7). Self-Care for Parents of Children with ADHD | Kids Empowered 4 Life. Kids Empowered 4 Life. https://kidsempowered4life.com/self-care-for-parents-of-children-with-adhd/

Accardo, A. L., Pontes, N. M. H., & Pontes, M. (2022). Heightened Anxiety and Depression Among Autistic Adolescents with ADHD: Findings From the National Survey of Children's Health 2016–2019. Journal of Autism and Developmental Disorders, 54(2), 563–576. https://doi.org/10.1007/s10803-022-05803-9

ADHD and co-occurring conditions - CHADD. (2019, January 4). CHADD. https://chadd.org/about-adhd/co-occuring-conditions/

Admin, & Admin. (2023, August 3). How lifestyle changes can Lessen the impact of ADHD. PinnacleCare. https://www.pinnaclecare.com/highlights/blog/lifestyle-changes-adhd-symptoms/

Allan, C. C., Ph.D. (2024, January 17). How Behavioral Therapy Targets Executive Dysfunction — with Positivity and Praise. ADDitude. https://www.additudemag.com/behavioral-therapy-for-executive-functioning-adhd/

Ames, H. (2023, May 25). Support groups for those with ADHD and their loved ones. https://www.medicalnewstoday.com/articles/adhd-support-groups#support-groups

Angel, T. (2023, November 1). Everything you need to know about ADHD. Healthline. https://www.healthline.com/health/adhd

Arky, B. (2023, October 30). Sensory processing issues explained. Child Mind Institute. https://childmind.org/article/sensory-processing-issues-explained/

Attention-Deficit/Hyperactivity Disorder. (n.d.). National Institute of Mental Health (NIMH). https://www.nimh.nih.gov/health/topics/attention-deficit-hyperactivity-disorder-adhd

Behavior Therapy for Behavior or Conduct Problems | CDC. (2021, September 23). Centers for Disease Control and Prevention. https://www.cdc.gov/childrensmentalhealth/parent-behavior-therapy.html

Behavior therapy for young children with ADHD | CDC. (2020, September 23). Centers for Disease Control and Prevention. https://www.cdc.gov/ncbddd/adhd/behavior-therapy.html

Behavior Therapy Recommended as First Line of Treatment for Young Children with ADHD - CHADD. (2022, March 15). CHADD. https://chadd.org/adhd-weekly/cdc-recommends-behavior-therapy-as-first-line-of-treatment-for-young-children-with-adhd/

Behavioral Therapy for Young Children - CHADD. (2018, May 15). CHADD. https://chadd.org/for-parents/behavioral-therapy-for-young-children/

Blum, K., Chen, A. L. C., Braverman, E. R., Comings, D. E., Chen, T. J. H., Arcuri, V., Blum, S. H., Downs, B. W., Waite, R. L., Notaro, A., Lubar, J. F., Williams, L., Prihoda, T. J., Palomo, T., & Oscar-Berman, M. (2008). Attention-deficit-hyperactivity disorder and reward deficiency syndrome. Neuropsychiatric Disease and Treatment, 893. https://doi.org/10.2147/ndt.s2627

Blythehinderliter. (2023, May 8). How to Create an Emotion Regulation Plan with Your Child - Camber Children's Mental Health. Camber Children's Mental Health. https://www.cambermentalhealth.org/2020/04/28/how-to-create-an-emotion-regulation-plan-with-your-child/

Brown, B. (2022, December 11). Why Structure and Consistency Are Important For Kids • Kids Creek Therapy. Kids Creek Therapy. https://www.kidscreektherapy.com/why-structure-and-consistency-are-important-for-kids/

Buzanko, C. (2022, March 19). ADDitude magazine: The Key to ADHD Emotional Regulation? Cultivating Gratitude, Pride & Compassion. Dr. Caroline Buzanko. https://drcarolinebuzanko.com/additude-magazine-the-key-to-adhd-emotional-regulation-cultivating-gratitude-pride-compassion/

Carroll, A. (2023, October 4). ADHD Is Not a Learning Disability (But it Does Affect Learning). ADDA - Attention Deficit Disorder Association. https://add.org/is-adhd-a-learning-disability/

Chung, W., Jiang, S., Paksarian, D., Nikolaidis, A., Castellanos, F. X., Merikangas, K. R., & Milham, M. P. (2019). Trends in the prevalence and incidence of Attention-Deficit/Hyperactivity Disorder among adults and children of different racial and ethnic groups. JAMA Network Open, 2(11), e1914344. https://doi.org/10.1001/jamanetworkopen.2019.14344

Dubai, L. D. N. I. (2024, February 4). Positive Parent-Child relationships: building trust and connection. The Little Dreamers Nursery. https://dreamersnursery.com/positive-parent-child-relationships/

DuPaul, G. J., Gormley, M. J., & Laracy, S. D. (2012). Comorbidity of LD and ADHD. Journal of Learning Disabilities, 46(1), 43–51. https://doi.org/10.1177/0022219412464351

Early signs of ADHD in children. (n.d.). HealthyChildren.org. https://www.healthychildren.org/English/health-issues/conditions/adhd/Pages/Early-Warning-Signs-of-ADHD.aspx

Evidence-Based Treatments for ADHD. (2023, November 7). The TAP Clinic. https://www.tapclinicnc.com/post/evidence-based-treatments-for-adhd

Executive Functioning Skills - The Pathway 2 success. (2022, August 13). The Pathway 2 Success. https://www.thepathway2success.com/executive-functioning-skills/

Faraone, S. V., Banaschewski, T., Coghill, D., Zheng, Y., Biederman, J., Bellgrove, M. A., Newcorn, J. H., Gignac, M., Saud, N. M. A., Manor, I., Rohde, L. A., Yang, L., Cortese, S., Almagor, D., Stein, M. A., Albatti, T. H., Al-Joudi, H. F., Alqahtani, M. M. J., Asherson, P., . . . Wang, Y. (2021). The World Federation of ADHD International Consensus Statement: 208 Evidence-based conclusions about the disorder. Neuroscience & Biobehavioral Reviews, 128, 789–818. https://doi.org/10.1016/j.neubiorev.2021.01.022

Faraone, S. V., & Larsson, H. (2018). Genetics of attention deficit hyperactivity disorder. Molecular Psychiatry, 24(4), 562–575. https://doi.org/10.1038/s41380-018-0070-0

Fast Facts: Preventing Bullying |Violence Prevention|Injury Center|CDC. (n.d.). https://www.cdc.gov/violenceprevention/youthviolence/bullyingresearch/fastfact.html

Flynn, L. (2024, February 1). *ADHD and emotional regulation.* OT4ADHD. https://ot4adhd.com/2023/03/13/adhd-and-emotional-regulation/ Friendship circle / resources. (2014, January 20). https://www.friendshipcircle.org/blog/2014/01/20/seven-organizations-that-provide-support-for-individuals-with-addadhd

Greenhill, L., MD. (2022, January 14). Advances in treatments for ADHD. Psychiatric Times. https://www.psychiatrictimes.com/view/advances-in-treatments-for-adhd

Greenwood, S. (2023, November 2). Views of the American family in 2023 are mixed | Pew Research Center. Pew Research Center's Social & Demographic Trends Project. https://www.pewresearch.org/social-trends/2023/09/14/public-has-mixed-views-on-the-modern-american-family/

Hargitai, L., Livingston, L. A., & Shah, P. (n.d.). ADHD more strongly linked to anxiety and depression compared to autism – new research. The Conversation. https://theconversation.com/adhd-more-strongly-linked-to-anxiety-and-depression-compared-to-autism-new-research-198040

How ADHD can affect your family. (2018, July 18). WebMD. https://www.webmd.com/add-adhd/childhood-adhd/adhd-effects-on-family

Is ADHD hereditary? - CHADD. (2018, May 8). CHADD. https://chadd.org/adhd-weekly/is-adhd-hereditary/

Jackson, L. (2022, August 26). 7 activities to teach patience to the child Who wants it NOW. Connected Families. https://connectedfamilies.org/teaching-children-wait-well/

Jones, H. (2024a, February 10). ADHD in Boys vs. Girls. Verywell Health. https://www.verywellhealth.com/do-adhd-symptoms-differ-in-boys-and-girls-5207995

Kinch, C. (2015, July 31). Environmental concentrations of contaminants affect morphological and neuroendocrine development in zebrafish. https://prism.ucalgary.ca/items/7deeea76-3328-4245-98a5-9e4e271bda3b

Kinman, T. (2016, March 22). Gender differences in ADHD symptoms. Healthline. https://www.healthline.com/health/adhd/adhd-symptoms-in-girls-and-boys

Koutsoklenis, A., & Honkasilta, J. (2023). ADHD in the DSM-5-TR: What has changed and what has not. Frontiers in Psychiatry, 13. https://doi.org/10.3389/fpsyt.2022.1064141

Lange, K. W., Reichl, S., Lange, K., Tucha, L., & Tucha, O. (2010). The history of attention deficit hyperactivity disorder. Adhd Attention Deficit and Hyperactivity Disorders, 2(4), 241–255. https://doi.org/10.1007/s12402-010-0045-8

Learning Disabilities Worldwide | Environmental Toxins. (n.d.). Learning Disabilities. https://www.ldworldwide.org/environmental-toxins

Lopatin, A. (2023, February 21). How to Nurture Connected Independence in Kids & Teens with ADHD: Parenting with the 5C's Framework. Dr. Sharon Saline. https://drsharonsaline.com/2022/03/16/how-to-nurture-connected-independence-in-kids-and-teens-with-adhd-parenting-with-the-5cs-framework/

Low, K. (2022, April 19). Why children with ADHD need structure and routines. Verywell Mind. https://www.verywellmind.com/why-is-structure-important-for-kids-with-adhd-20747

Métraux, J. (2022, August 18). What does your gut have to do with ADHD? EverydayHealth.com. https://www.everydayhealth.com/adhd/gut-health-and-adhd-is-there-a-link/

Mittal, S., Bax, A., Blum, N. J., Shults, J., Barbaresi, W. J., Cacia, J., Deavenport-Saman, A., Friedman, S., LaRosa, A., Loe, I. M., Tulio, S., Vanderbilt, D., & Harstad, E. (2023). Receipt of Behavioral Therapy in Preschool-Age Children with ADHD and Coexisting Conditions: A DBPNet Study. Journal of Developmental and Behavioral Pediatrics, 44(9), e651–e656. https://doi.org/10.1097/dbp.0000000000001216

Morin, A. (2023, December 13). 8 common myths about ADHD. Understood. https://www.understood.org/articles/common-myths-about-adhd

Nigg, J. T., Elmore, A. L., Natarajan, N., Friderici, K. H., & Nikolas, M. A. (2015). Variation in an iron metabolism gene moderates the association between blood lead levels and Attention-Deficit/Hyperactivity disorder in children. Psychological Science, 27(2), 257–269. https://doi.org/10.1177/0956797615618365

Parent education: Confusing ADHD and LD: They are not the same thing! (n.d.). https://www.foothillsacademy.org/community/articles/confusing_adhd_and_ld

Patino, E. (2024, January 4). Biofeedback: What you need to know. Understood. https://www.understood.org/articles/biofeedback-what-it-is-and-how-it-works

Philadelphia, C. H. O. (2020, July 9). Tips for Keeping Kids with ADHD Organized. Children's Hospital of Philadelphia. https://www.chop.edu/news/health-tip/tips-for-keeping-kids-with-adhd-organized

Pierce, R. (2024, March 3). Supporting a sibling with executive functioning challenges: tips and strategies | Life Skills Advocate. Life Skills Advocate. https://lifeskillsadvocate.com/blog/supporting-a-sibling-with-executive-functioning-challenges/

Psychiatrist.com. (2023, April 6). ADHD risk influenced by gut microbiome | Psychiatrist.com. https://www.psychiatrist.com/news/adhd-risk-influenced-by-gut-microbiome/

R, K. (2023a, February 21). *Cooling Down Conversations in Neurodiverse Families: De-escalate and do-over with 'WAIT-Now' and 'Take Back of the Day'* Dr. Sharon Saline. https://drsharonsaline.com/2021/09/07/cooling-down-conversations-in-neurodiverse-families/

R, K. (2023b, February 21). Negative Memory Bias and ADHD: Tips to Help Kids and Youth with ADHD Remember the Positives. Dr. Sharon Saline. https://drsharonsaline.com/2021/07/07/negative-memory-bias-and-adhd-tips-to-help-kids-and-youth-with-adhd-remember-the-positives/

Roth, E. (2023, May 19). What are the 3 types of ADHD? Healthline. https://www.healthline.com/health/adhd/three-types-adhd

Rouse, M. H., Ph.D. (2023, November 6). How can we help kids with Self-Regulation? Child Mind Institute. https://childmind.org/article/can-help-kids-self-regulation/

Rudy, L. J. (2023, July 20). Autism vs. ADHD: What Are the Differences? Verywell Health. https://www.verywellhealth.com/autism-vsadhd-5213000

Russell, L. (2024, March 1). 5 ADHD strengths to harness in your child. They Are the Future. https://www.theyarethefuture.co.uk/adhd-strengths-in-your-child/

ScB, S. R. (2023, June 5). Helping children who are neurodiverse build friendships. Harvard Health. https://www.health.harvard.edu/blog/helping-children-who-are-neurodiverse-build-friendships-202304052909

Sharon. (2023, February 21). ADHD, Emotional Regulation and Managing Family Conflict: Replacing Time-outs with Time-in or Time-apart. Dr. Sharon Saline. https://drsharonsaline.com/2021/11/16/adhd-emotional-regulation-and-managing-family-conflict-replacing-time-outs-with-time-in-or-time-apart/

Shuai, L., Daley, D., Wang, Y., Zhang, J., Kong, Y., Tan, X., & Ji, N. (2017). Executive Function Training for Children with Attention Deficit Hyperactivity Disorder. Chinese Medical Journal, 130(5), 549–558. https://doi.org/10.4103/0366-6999.200541

Story, J. (2024, February 29). The ADHD body double: a unique tool for getting things done. ADDA - Attention Deficit Disorder Association. https://add.org/the-body-double/

Strecker, D. (2023, October 14). 12 Ways to Improve your child's confidence. https://www.linkedin.com/pulse/12-ways-improve-your-childs-confidence-denny-strecker-nmnbc/

Symptoms and diagnosis of ADHD | CDC. (2022, July 26). Centers for Disease Control and Prevention. https://www.cdc.gov/ncbddd/adhd/diagnosis.html

The ADHD Diagnostic Process - CHADD. (2018, May 14). CHADD. https://chadd.org/for-professionals/the-adhd-diagnostic-process/

The exercise prescription for ADHD - CHADD. (2018, July 20). CHADD. https://chadd.org/attention-article/the-exercise-prescription-for-adhd/

Treatment and management. (n.d.). https://www.aafp.org/family-physician/patient-care/prevention-wellness/emotional-wellbeing/adhd-toolkit/treatment-and-management.html

Treatment of ADHD | CDC. (2020, September 21). Centers for Disease Control and Prevention. https://www.cdc.gov/ncbddd/adhd/treatment.html

Understanding Emotional Development - CHADD. (2023, January 20). CHADD. https://chadd.org/attention-article/understanding-emotional-development/

Use summer to improve your Parent-Child relationship - CHADD. (2019, July 18). CHADD. https://chadd.org/adhd-weekly/use-summer-to-improve-your-parent-child-relationship/

What is ADHD? (2021, January 26). Centers for Disease Control and Prevention. https://www.cdc.gov/ncbddd/adhd/facts.html

Wilkins, F., & Nikolaidis, A., Ph.D. (2024, March 1). How is the ADHD brain different? Child Mind Institute. https://childmind.org/article/how-is-the-adhd-brain-different/

Printed in Great Britain
by Amazon

47636893R00086